Overlords of Mexico

"Wander, look for lands . . . send pioneers ahead, have them plant maize, when the harvest is ready, move up to it—keep me, Huitzilopochtli, always with you, carrying me like a banner, feed me on human hearts torn from the recently sacrificed . . ."

The Aztec did as their god commanded. They conquered and sacrificed, planted and reaped. And in so doing they created a form of life whose luxury has never been equalled by any of the other peoples of America.

Victor W. von Hagen, scientist and writer, explores the fabulous Aztec world in this richly illustrated book. He covers the whole of their complex civilization—from the political and social structure of their democratic city-state to their method of preparing human beings for religious sacrifice. He tells how the Aztec made war and conquest the basic pattern of their daily life. He analyzes their advanced forms of art, writing and sculpture. And he describes their temples and palaces, particularly the splendor of Moctezuma's kingdom, the lavish city of Tenochtitlán, built in the midst of a salt lake, deep in the interior of Mexico.

This fascinating history of the Aztec, a tribe of people who forever left their impress on the continent of America, is illustrated with eight pages of photographs. It also features 55 drawings by Alberto Beltrán, winner of the Pan-American Prize (the first prize for drawing) in the First Biennial of Painting and Drawing sponsored by the Univedsidad Nacional of Mexico.

Other Books by VICTOR W. von HAGEN

EXPLORATION:

Off with Their Heads (1937)
Ecuador the Unknown (1938)
Jungle in the Clouds (1940)
Ecuador and the Galápagos Islands (1949)
Highway of the Sun (1955)

BIOGRAPHY:

South America Called Them (La Condamine, Humboldt, Darwin, Spruce) (1945)
Maya Explorer, The Life of John Lloyd Stephens (1947)
Frederick Catherwood: Architect (1950)
The Four Seasons of Manuela (1952)

ARCHAEOLOGY—ANTHROPOLOGY

The Tsatchela Indians of Western Ecuador (1939)
The Jicaque Indians of Honduras (1943)
The Maya and Aztec Papermakers (1943)
Realm of the Incas (1957; MP355)
World of the Maya (1960; MP394)
Ancient Sun Kingdoms of the Americas (1961)
Incas, People of the Sun (1961)

ACKNOWLEDGMENTS

The author wishes to thank the following publishers for their kind permission to reprint from the books indicated below:

Farrar, Straus & Giroux, Inc.: *The Discovery and Conquest of Mexico, 1517-1521,* by Bernal Díaz del Castillo, translated by A. P. Maudslay. Copyright 1956 by Farrar, Straus and Cudahy, Inc.

Routledge & Kegan Paul Ltd.: *The Discovery and Conquest of Mexico, 1517-1521,* by Bernal Díaz del Castillo, translated by A. P. Maudslay; and *Five Letters, 1519-1526,* by Hernando Cortés, translated by J. Bayard Morris.

Harper & Brothers: *Beyond the Mexique Bay,* by Aldous Huxley.

MENTOR BOOKS are published by
The New American Library, Inc.
1301 Avenue of the Americas, New York, New York 10019

PRINTED IN THE UNITED STATES OF AMERICA

The AZTEC:
Man and Tribe

Victor Wolfgang von Hagen

ILLUSTRATED BY
ALBERTO BELTRÁN

REVISED EDITION

MENTOR: ANCIENT CIVILIZATIONS
PUBLISHED BY THE NEW AMERICAN LIBRARY

"Is there such a thing as an impartial history? And what is history? The written representation of past events. But what is an event. . . . It is a notable fact. Now, how is the historian to discriminate whether a fact is notable or no? He decides this arbitrarily, according to his character and idiosyncrasy, at his own taste and fancy—in a word, as an artist. . . ."

ANATOLE FRANCE, *The Garden of Epicurus*

FOR MY GRANDSON
PHILIPPE EVARISTE VICTOR BORDAZ
FUTURE ARCHAEOLOGIST

CONTENTS

List of Illustrations

FIGURES

PLATES

I

The Historical and Geographical Background

1. Of Archaeological Explorers—and Time

THE AZTECS, of course, did not call themselves "Aztecs." And very definitely they were not an empire. Moreover they arrived so late on the Mexican scene and were so unimportant when they did come to the lakes, which was Mexico, that not a single tribe recorded their arrival. Their "kings" were in reality elected "speakers" and there were no "halls of Montezuma" (except in song), so that the misconception of there being an "Aztec Empire" is actually a non sequitur of history just as was in fact the Holy Roman Empire (which was neither holy, Roman, nor an empire).

Still the Tenochas, called "Aztecs," were the first of the ancient Sun Kingdoms to be made known to the other world and the first to tumble into Europe's lap, and with this dramatic impact on man's imagination the first impressions cannot be undone; we remain stuck with the "Aztec Empire."

How and why this barbaric American Sun Kingdom fell into the hands of a relatively few *conquistadores* is a twice-told tale; still no matter how often retold, it never loses its wonderment—how "stout Cortez" made his way into the heartland of Tenochtitlán, seized its "king" and forced it to accept a *pax hispaniensis*.[19]

The literature on the Aztecs is simply overwhelming. There seems not a phase of their life that has not been explored, analyzed and written up; their origins, history, and rebus

11

writing, their religion and calendar, have been gone over again and again; that which remains of their glyph scripts has been published; excavations within and outside the traditional "Aztec Empire" territory are being carried out progressively; for more than two decades reports, well documented and learned, continue to be issued at a rate that is truly astounding. For almost two hundred years some of the great names in literature have written on the Aztecs and their neighbors—and when all of this is seen together in one library it is so formidable in quantity and quality that it would seem almost an impertinence for anyone to write another account of the Aztecs. And yet. . . .

And yet since the Aztecs arrived so very late on the Mexican scene (there were so many cultures before them), and since they were magicbound every moment of their lives—peopling their world with gods and symbols—there has remained in the literature much that is bewildering, so that it is pertinent for their story to be told in human terms. More: since the history of the Aztecs (which involves mythology, astronomy, ethnology, and search into all that went on thousands of years before them) is complicated, it is not always an easy subject to write on or to read about.

There is very little in this life that is definitive, and there is seldom a book that exhausts a subject, particularly one so involved as the Aztecs. The old Roman who said on his deathbed that "much remains to be done and much will still remain nor shall any man after the revolution of a thousand ages be denied the opportunity of contributing something" could well have been speaking of the Aztecs. A concise new account of them does not have to make any apology.

There is now no lack of literary ammunition for it. It was the plaint of William Prescott when he began to write his celebrated *History of the Conquest of Mexico* in 1839 [67] that he had to cast his cannons before he fired them, meaning that he had to create his own holograph library by having all the unpublished manuscripts copied in Spain before he could begin. Such is far from the situation now—the material at one's disposal is awesome.

The Spanish conquerors of the Aztecs were for the most part lettered and literate and they felt the historicity of the moment. Hernán Cortés, who reported history as he made it, was, for his time, considered to be a man of learning; he had attended the University of Salamanca. His famous *Five Letters* [21] to his King-Emperor, written between the intervals of battle, are as alive as if printed in blood. There were others, too, who wrote of the conquest while the flesh of history was still warm. An "Anonymous Conqueror" [7] wrote a *Narrative of Some Things of New Spain and of the Great City of Temestitan*; another, one Andres de Tapia, who involved himself as much with women as with conquest, left his literary impressions of the fall of the Aztecs, a book which pushed him up as it pulled his captain, Cortés, down.[78] The most literary of the chroniclers, Francisco López de Gómara, penned his *Chronicle of the Conquest of New Spain*,[54] and as he was the household chaplain to Cortés, then Marquis of the Valley and full of riches and renown, he blew the glorification of Cortés theme so one-sidedly that it set an old war horse of the conquest, Bernal Díaz del Castillo ("I am now an old man, over eighty-four years of age, and I have lost my sight and hearing . . ."), to dictating his wonderful and ageless *The Discovery and Conquest of Mexico*.[25]

The crusading padres continued the literature where the soldiers left off. In their efforts to effect the change within Mexico from one mythology to another, they perforce studied the languages, the myths, and the round of daily life of the peoples. The most indefatigable of these was Bernardino de Sahagún,[68] who arrived in Mexico in 1529 and who left, after decades of devoted study, a history of the life and times of a people that is invaluable to any who work on the Aztecs. And there were many others. The literature is deepened because of them as well as by such as Dr. Francisco Hernández, a physician sent out by the King of Spain to examine the new plants of the "newfound world"; his five-year plant exploration with the aid of numerous native scribes and artists is one of the great monuments of botanical science [36] and from it we have a wonderful glimpse into Aztec earth-knowledge.

The seventeenth century belonged to the padres; it was the period of printed vocabularies, dictionaries of Indian languages, breviaries, and a sort of demi-history—a literature they termed *relaciones*. But the eighteenth century brought the Enlightenment and with it an interest in the past, the sort of romantic speculation that appears in Count Volney's rhapsodic elegy to *Les Ruines*.[83] The learned world made much over symbols; the romantic agony was at hand and intellectual interest was rekindled in the remains of the "Aztec Empire."

The youthful Alexander von Humboldt arrived in Mexico in 1803 after four years of strenuous exploration in South

America, and with him and *Les Ruines,* the whole of the
then available Mexican archaeological material was recast in
a modern scientific mold. In 1810 he published, in one handsome folio, the first good reproductions of "American" art.[40]

In England, Edward King, Viscount Kingsborough, who
had never seen an American Indian in his life—nor wanted
to (for he had already preconceived Indians as having originated out of the wandering tribes of Israel)—was publishing
nine folio volumes of reproductions of all the known glyph
writings of the Maya and Aztec to prove his "American
Indians are Jews" theory.[48] It cost him his fortune and his
life. But by 1843 William Prescott had given the Indians
back to the Indians by the publication of his *History of the
Conquest of Mexico.*

Since then no one nation has had a Mexican monopoly. The
North Americans, beginning with John Lloyd Stephens and
William Prescott, have continued on uninterruptedly for a
century; the late George Vaillant, Samuel Lothrop, Matthew
Stirling, and Gordon Ekholm, to mention only a few, continue the tradition. The British have never been far behind;
they have maintained the line from Frederick Catherwood
to A. P. Maudslay, from Zelia Nuttall to T. A. Joyce.[46] It
continues with C. A. Burland of the British Museum who
carries on the inheritance. The Swedes were also interested
in Mexico long before the comparative studies of Baron
Erland Nordenskiöld were published; now Sigvald Linné continues it.

The Germans have been active in the Mexican field ever
since Humboldt wrote his first book and brought back to
Berlin its first glimpse of Mexican glyph writing; from Eduard
Seler to Ernst Förstemann (who helped decipher the Maya
glyphs) to Hermann Beyer (who gave much substance to the
theoretical studies), the interest and quality of scholarship
have been continuous; Paul Kirchhoff [49] maintains it at the
present day. The French have been interested since back in
1529, when André Thévet, cosmographer to the King of
France, studied the Mexican Tribute Charts which a pirate
had pocketed as his part of the rape of the Spanish convoy
off Vera Cruz. From the 1840s, when the gentle aristocratic scholar Comte Adolphe de Circourt gave William
Prescott aid, until the present-day scholarly work of Jacques
Soustelle [74] (mentioned often in this book), the French have
been stimulated by *le Mexicain.*

These last archaeological years have belonged to the Mexican scholars. New ruins have been found, restored, and in-

vestigated; careful stratigraphical work with advanced techniques has been carried out. The names of the Mexicans who have shown this wonderful capacity to examine their past are so many that a mere recitation of them all would sound like a bibliography—Manuel Gamio, Alfonso Caso, José García Payón, Eduardo Noguera, Ignacio Marquina, to mention only a few—and books, pamphlets, papers, constantly flow out of all this archaeological activity. The result is that the date of emergence of early man in Mexico is continually being pushed back.

All this activity has given rise to a general interest in everything that has formed man's past (for the past is contained in the present just as the properties of a triangle are involved in its definition) and there has been much public interest in the literature. Unfortunately, to have a generous panorama requires lengthy and involved reading. And so while the general reader would like to know something of all this, still the sheer bulk of the material . . .

I have tried to determine, in my manner, the essential quality of the Aztec and put it down in such a literary form as to attract, and not to frighten off before it instructs, the general and curious reader. Throughout I have aimed at simplicity with the object of following the advice of Anatole France, who said to a young writer: "I begin to ask myself whether supreme talent may not consist of writing very simply about very complicated matters."

2. The Setting

ALL MEXICO is divided into two parts: the moun-
tainous and the flat.

The land is one of extremes: the contrasts of the volcanic
wastes, the high *mesetas* of thin air, the aridity of deserts, the
lush parts folding one upon another, exiling valley from
valley, has made this land the love and despair of man ever
since he took possession of this Mexican earth.

If a figure must be devised for it, Mexico is shaped like a
cornucopia, from the broad open tablelands of its northern
boundaries, where bison once roamed, down a thousand
miles south to the narrow isthmus where the land tumbles
into mountains and tropical verdure with all the luxuriant
richness that is centered there, where the Indians found jade,
coral, shells, chocolate, amber, rubber, quetzal plumes—the
paradise lands to the mountainbound dweller.

Mexico has extremes in climate, and, even though half the
land lies in the tropical zone, altitude is more important than
latitude. The eastern coast is broader and fiercely rained on
by the trade winds; it is more lush, and it was the ground for
early civilizations—the land of the Olmecs, Totonacs, Huastecs. The western coast has a narrower fringe of coast line:
nature here is not so prodigal and this is reflected in the early
cultures; they are threadbare compared to those on the
"other side."

The Mexican land rises up from these two shores, sometimes
abruptly, sometimes gradually, to the high plateau which is
the bulk of the geography of Mexico. Orizaba, a snow-
topped mountain (the Aztecs called it "Citlal-tépetl":
"Mountain of the Star"), rises out of the verdured jungle
to dominate at 18,000 feet the "cold lands." Here there is the
naked misery of soil that the first Spaniards found: ". . . three
days' march through a desert land uninhabitable on account
of its barrenness, lack of water, and great cold. . . . Oh! the

1. *The distribution of pre-Aztec tribes and cultures throughout Central Mexico and Guatemala-Yucatán. The Aztec came into cultural being in the part occupied by the Toltec.*

thirst and hunger suffered by the men assailed by whirl-winds of hailstones and rain." [21]

This high mesa land, varying between 3,000 and 10,000 feet, is classic Mexican soil. It has a troubled geology. Volcanoes in times past and continuing up into the present have belched out stone and pumice, tufa and obsidian, transforming much of what could have been fertile valleys into desert wastes. Nature has given Mexico some of the most spectacular scenery in the world, but it has extracted a heavy toll from man who has lived there. There are few navigable rivers; much of the land mass is made sterile by the volcanic outpourings; there are long, dry winters when dust storms carry off the loam and flash floods complete the ruin; there are high semidesert areas which are covered with the thickets of chaparral—cactus, mesquite, and sage. Then this direful aspect is replaced, in another region, with pine forests, and, when the land dips down into a watered zone, there are verdant, exuberant valleys.

Mexico had no Nile-like valley. It had no oases such as appear along the two-thousand-mile-long Peruvian coast to provide an eternal loam even in a rainless land; it had no burden animals—not even the llama. The wheel, had the Mexicans had it, would have done them no good as all is up and down, and high valley is walled from high valley almost throughout the length and breadth of the land; its heights are only passable to foot traffic.

Rain defines the seasons. On the high Mexican tableland it falls, the gods willing, between June and September; the rest of the months are dry except for a caprice of nature, and then it will fall out of season and may even snow in Mexico City, an event often recorded by the Aztec in their glyph history of unusual events.

The gifts of sun and rain not being equal, much of the land has been inhospitable to man. So while Mexico is vast, much of it in ancient times was empty of man and the empty places were where the soil was naked and sterile. The really fertile areas had been occupied since the earliest times, especially that incunabula of cultures, the valley of Anáhuac, the "land on the edge of the water," where Mexico City lies.

2. *Tenochtitlán as the Spaniards first saw it from the high-road that crossed the volcanic ridges surrounding the plateau of Mexico. Today a dry plain, it was a lake at that time.*

Where the mountains rise high in the center of the high Mexican plateau, where the cone of Popocatépetl rears snow-crowned, and beside it the reclining white-woman mountain, Ixtaccihuatl, there is a series of intermontane basins. These begin many miles northward around the fish-filled lakes of Michoacán and form a series of lagoons and lakes culminat-

ing about these snow-covered mountains in the valley of
Anáhuac. Great civilizations sprang out of this soil; the
Toltec, who left behind their immense "Place of the Gods"
at Teotihuacán, and the related culture of Tula, farther to the
north. The land height being less than 8,000 feet, corn, the
essential, grew here, as did much of the other needed things;
maguey was plentiful for fibers and the sweetish syrup
from which the pulque intoxicant is prepared; the saline lakes
yielded salt, a primary basic need for cereal-eating peoples.
The volcanoes erupting for untold centuries had piled up
layer upon layer, forming inexhaustible rock quarries, source
of the obsidian glass which when split became knives, weapons, and razors, and when polished, mirrors; and, for sculpture, a hard gray volcanic stone, capable of being chipped;
and a peculiar porous stuff, *tezontli,* usable for building
material.

Everything has its reasons—whether they are geographical
or sociological. Imperialist cultures were born out of the
harsh lands. In the tropic lands where man luxuriated in
warmth and sensualism, the expansion mood was limited,
but the man who came out of the high country, scoured by
wind and hail, was the one with imperialistic ambitions—an
effect of geography.

As the Incas in Peru, so the Aztecs of Mexico; they came
from the raw, colder zones. By the time the Aztecs emerged
as a tribe (circa A.D. 1200), the best lands were already occupied. They called themselves "Tenochas," descendants of
northern tribes. In their search for land they had to run the
gamut of numerous other peoples, already settled, who disputed passage with them. The hard necessity of war breeds
men; peoples grow by and against other peoples to inward
greatness, and the Aztecs were landless. They were, as others
had been before them, far-ranging animals wandering from
necessity—certainly in search of land but also perhaps just
out of the "primary microcosmic urgency to move." [75]

So into the lakes of Anáhuac in their year Ome-Acatl,
2-Reed (1168), moved this god-tormented tribe, this "Aztec"
people who were to systematize rapine and war into a tribute
state and forever leave their impress on the Mexican land.

3. The Year of the Spaniard

WHAT ARE the imponderables (called the genius) of a people that propel them forward and upward?

In 1168—a date fully accepted by historians—the Tenochas entered the lakes of Anáhuac from the northwest. Landless and friendless and already eyed with dismay by the other tribes settled about the lakes because of their readiness to offer human hearts to their gods, they had little of the outward trappings of human culture. A tribe small in numbers, composed of contending clans and forced out of one settled region after another, they finally selected several islets two miles out in Lake Texcoco and, carrying their god's image before them, they began in 1325 to build their city-state.

Within two centuries they were the overlords of Mexico, and Tenochtitlán, the "Place of the Tenocha," was the most sumptuous city ever raised by indigenous man in the Americas. The Spaniards, who had arrived to make its conquest and add its land titles to those of their Emperor-King, Charles V of Spain, entered "the great city of Tenochtitlán, Mexico, on the 8th of November . . . 1519."

"Gazing on such wonderful sights," wrote Bernal Díaz del Castillo remembering it vividly after fifty years, "we did not know what to say or what appeared before us was real." They proceeded along a "Causeway . . . eight paces in width" which ran "two miles from the mainland to the city . . . so crowded with people that there was hardly room for them all . . . the towers were full of people . . . canoes [came] from all parts of the lake."

Being close to the entrance of the city, they were met by the "king's" entourage: the Great Moctezuma got down from his litter and, supported by others, continued "beneath a marvellously rich canopy of green coloured feathers with much gold and silver embroidery and with pearls and [jade] suspended from a sort of bordering, which was wonderful to look at. The Great Moctezuma was richly attired . . . many other lords . . . walked before [him], sweeping the ground where he would tread and spreading cloths on it . . ."

As they entered the city they were hardly able to believe their eyes. Bernal Díaz remembered that he "could [not] count the multitude of men and women and boys who were in the streets . . . in canoes on the canals, who had come out to see us. It was indeed wonderful, and, now that I am writing about it"—he was then eighty-four—"it all comes before my eyes as though it had happened but yesterday."

Put to rest in "great halls and chambers canopied with the cloth of the country," they soon visited the Uei Tlatoani, the "Chief Speaker," Moctezuma, in his own immense quarters. Moctezuma lived in Lucullan luxury. "They prepared more than three hundred plates of the food that Moctezuma was going to eat . . . such a variety of dishes . . . so numerous that I cannot finish naming them . . . Four very beautiful cleanly women brought water for his hands . . . other women brought him tortilla bread . . . He was served on Cholula earthenware . . . From time to time they brought him, in cup-shaped vessels of pure gold, a certain drink made from cacao . . ."

Later Bernal Díaz del Castillo accompanied Cortés and looked at the stored treasures of this tribute-state and into where Moctezuma "kept the accounts of all the revenue . . . in his books which were made of paper which they call *amatl,* and he had a great house full of these books." And they saw the storehouses of cereals and maize, beans and peppers, brought in as tribute, other storehouses full of war dress, "many of them richly adorned with gold and precious stones," and arms and shields and "a sort of broadswords ¾ . . . like to hand-swords set with stone [obsidian] knives which cut much better than our very own swords," and bows and arrows stacked to the high ceiling and "artful shields . . . made so that they can be rolled up . . . and quilted cotton armour."

There was a royal aviary of which Bernal Díaz said: ". . . I am forced to abstain from enumerating every kind of bird that was there . . . from the Royal Eagle . . . down to tiny birds of many-coloured plumage . . . from which they take rich plumage which they use in their green feather work. All the birds . . . breed in these houses . . . each kind of bird has its proper food . . . and two hundred men and women to attend them. . . ."

There were the lapidaries, "the skilled workmen Mocte-zuma employed in every craft that was practised among

3. *The valley of Anáhuac and the lakes of Mexico.*

Although they have five names, the lakes were actually a continuous body of water. Since there was no outlet, the water was mostly saline except in the southern parts (lakes Chalco and Xochimilco) which received fresh streams of water from the snow-topped volcanoes. The system of dikes and causeways was later developed by the Aztec so as to control the salinity of the lakes.

them," and "workers in gold and silver" whose wares even the great goldsmiths in Spain were forced to admire (and Albrecht Dürer, also; see pages 13, 155. Then there were those who polished precious stones and jades and "the great craftsmen in feather work, and painters and sculptors . . . the Indian women who did the weaving . . . who made such an immense quantity of fine fabrics with wonderful feather work designs . . ."

The public markets, of which there were four in the city, were dominated by the great market place at Tlaltelolco, and "we were astounded at the number of people and the quantity of merchandise that it contained, and at the good order and control that was maintained . . . Each kind of merchandise was kept by itself and had its fixed place marked out. . . . [There were] dealers in gold, silver, and precious stones, feathers, mantles, and embroidered goods." Then "Indian slaves both men and women" which they brought into the "great market for sale as the Portuguese bring negroes from Guinea . . . tied to long poles, with collars round their necks . . . Next . . . traders who sold great pieces of cloth and cotton . . . and [those] who sold cacao." There was coarse cloth from the maguey fibers, sandals from the plant fiber. In another part "there were skins of tigers and lions, of otters and jackals, deer . . ."

And "those who sold beans . . . vegetables . . . fowls, cocks with wattles . . . hares, deer . . . young dogs—the eating variety—and every sort of pottery made in a thousand different forms . . . those who sold honey and honey paste . . . lumber, boards . . . beams, blocks . . . and the vendors of *ocote* firewood . . ."

"Truly, my Lord," wrote Hernán Cortés, continuing the description of this fabulous city when eloquence had failed Bernal Díaz, "Truly, my Lord . . . the great city of Tenochtitlán . . . built in the midst of this salt lake, two leagues from any point in the mainland, is connected by four causeways . . . twelve feet wide . . . the city is as large as Seville or Cordova . . . as for the whole, it is so large I am unable to find out exactly the extent of Moctezuma's kingdom. . . ."

All this—to which, despite its rather Arabian Nights unreality, archaeology has now fully attested—was what the Spaniards found, a luxuriant form of life of a kind which no other people in the Americas had ever attained.

How had it all come about?

The answer—better the explanation—lies in the cultural history that had long preceded the Aztec.

4. Man Comes to the Americas

No one knows precisely how early it was that man first migrated to the Americas. That man arrived as Man, that he did not grow out of any subhuman present in this continent (there was none), all are in agreement. But how did he arrive? Did he come socially matured, a cultural beast full-blown from the brows of Outer Asia—why, asked Herodotus in irritation, must the continents always be named after women?—casually wandering into the new land while following the spoor of mammals across that high bourn, the Aleutian land bridge from Outer Mongolia to the Americas; or did he come in a series of migrations over a long period of time from his Asiatic spawning grounds, sufficiently conscious of "something" out there, and continue these treks century upon century? Or did he come self-propelled in fragile open dugouts across these agitated seas and arrive fully accoutered in cultural panoply to impose himself on his dim-witted cousins earlier arrived?

No one really knows. And the controversy is as old as the discovery of the Americas. The omniscient Church collided at once with reality. If the flood as detailed in the Bible was true, if it destroyed all mankind except Noah and his chosen family to repopulate the earth, how did these Americans get to that continent, and, moreover, who were they? Where theologic logic failed, dialectics was triumphant: the Indians of course were Jews—one of the lost tribes of Israel. There are many labored tracts on this theme, written by the first padres in America.[32] One Fray Diego Durán—the rational part of whose pioneer work in Mexico is used often in this book—wrote that "the supposition is confirmed . . . these natives are of the Ten Tribes of Israel that Salmanassar, King of the Assyrians, made prisoner and carried to Assyria in the time of Hoshea, King of Israel." The Church may have resolved God's anthropology but had not settled it among the philosophers; the famous Huig de Groot, pioneer of international law, believed in the seventeenth century that the North American Indians were Scandinavian, the Peruvians,

24

4. *The origin of man in America.*

Chinese, and the Brazilians, African. He was immediately answered by his countryman Johannes de Laet, who was stirred to great rage over so inept a deduction. Anyone, he wrote, except a dunderpate could see that the American savages were in reality—Scythians. By this time writers of Cromwellian England were involved in the controversy. Thomas Thoroughgood claimed that he had heard from a rabbi in Holland, who had been entertained by a community of Jews in Peru, that the Indians practiced circumcisional rites; that was all the evidence that he needed to compose his pamphlet *Jewes in America*. But he was soon challenged by another writer, whose tract was entitled *Americans no Jewes*.

So it has gone on through the centuries. Edward King, Viscount Kingsborough, was a victim of it. The Church of the Latter-day Saints, whose sacred Book of Mormon traces this genealogy, even today finances with "Golden Tablets of Moroni" highly equivocal research to support the theory that the American Indian is a descendant of one of the tribes of Israel.[73]

Anthropologists would be delighted to have so simple an explanation of the peopling of the Americas; instead of which . . .

Instead of which there are many theories and of sufficient variety to fit anyone's wishing. The theory that has long prevailed in anthropological circles is that man came out of Asia more than forty thousand years ago, abysmally primitive and in the early neolithic stage * of development, and his culture was arrived at by independent invention in the new American land. The wave of land migrations stopped after climatic change and after the Bering Strait "land bridge," subject then as now to constant earthquakes with upheavals and subsidences, finally sank under Arctic waters.

This theory, upon which archaeological theories pyramided, is under siege from many quarters; archaeologists, botanists, geographers have attacked it as untenable. There are fifty "strikingly similar" features between Pacific island cultures and those of America, only to be explained by trans-Pacific diffusions. The "diffusionists" insist that crossings between the continents, by raft, ship, or outrigger, appear to have been numerous. Even though there is no proof, these theories have subsisted on the basis of faith, and now in the last years, of passionate feeling. But a feeling does not adduce its reasons. It has none; they must be lent to it. There is no positive proof on either side of the anthropological fence. Arguments, weighty and frivolous, are many. This has led one British scientist to conclude that "however, the cogency of such arguments, and there are [good ones] on both sides, is not generally accepted as convincing and it may be perhaps admitted that the position taken on either side is fortified by faith. . . ."

However, until someone comes along with facts that can be weighed in the balance, the American Indian had his cultural beginnings *here*. Early Neolithic man was a land wanderer, not a seafarer; he followed the spoor of animals and he came out of Asia over a land bridge which had been used for aeons of time by the mammals. So, in keeping with the opening leitmotif, which allows me to select "according to my character and idiosyncrasy, at my own taste and fancy—in a word, as an artist," it came about in this manner:

It was the end of the Ice Age and a new world was forming. The glacial ice that had held the world in eternal winter was melting and pouring brawling streams of frigid

---

* The Neolithic or New Stone Age is the period when men began to be food producers (after 5000 B.C.); before that was the Mesolithic, (10,000 B.C.) when he was a hunter and fisher; as Paleolithic man (15,000 B.C.) he was a food-gatherer and occasional hunter. All of the early cultures in the Fertile Crescent of the Near East, Sumerian, Egyptian, etc., were Neolithic.

water into the agitated ocean. Plants that had survived pushed their pallid heads out of the tundra; spores of seeds, wafted on the streams of warmer air, found root, and, under the climatic change, rank luxuriance gradually usurped the place of ice. Over the face of this strange new green earth, after long periods of evolutionary progress, man, *real* man, appeared. He is not out of the pale of world memory; three hundred centuries ago he was making zoomorphic engravings on the walls of caves, creditable intaglios of bison, mammoths, deer, wolves. In body he was a completely formed type; he had wit, ornament, and a technique of living. The massive herds of mammals that roamed the earth soon made the acquaintance of this tool-using primate. He followed them, flowing around the Mediterranean and crossing it. He wandered through the wilderness of the Nile into the sylvan lands of India, Java, China, and throughout the whole of Eurasia. Finally he broke into that world-in-itself, Mongolia.

Slow century followed slow century and the metamorphoses of time were making changes in this primitive man —the descendants of the *pithecanthropi* were becoming distinct peoples. These Siberian dwellers had black, coarse hair and straight, flat, beardless faces with cheekbones in prominence and eyes indexed by the epicanthic fold. They were already, at this time, using stone celts for tools. Some of them then mutated out from their world and moved into an utterly new one: forty thousand years ago, these men with the Mongoloid eyes, following the northern paths of mammals, made the first invasion of the Americas.

Primitive man came to America over its roof. Westward from Alaska are twelve hundred miles of islands. The geologic residue of volcanic action, they stretch out in an endless chain across the Bering Sea within sight of outer Siberia. Once they were a land bridge, a connecting link between continents, and over them for countless ages had surged herds of proto-camels, proto-tapirs, and mammoth elephants crossing over from America.

It was the end of the Ice Age when this man came to America. We know of his presence, for he has left his bones commingled in fossilized death with extinct animals. Throughout the centuries following this migration these people moved down the unglaciated Alaskan corridor into the vast land theaters of America. Within five centuries they penetrated the most remote corners of the hemisphere, from icebound north to icebound south, covering eventually

America's entire 135 degrees of latitude. Living here on the shores of frozen or tropical waters, at altitudes varying from sea level to several thousands of feet, living there in forest, grassy plains, or deserts; here starved, there in plenty; here with a night of six months' duration, there a night twelve hours long; here among health-giving winds, there cursed with disease—ancient man in America, greatly varying in his cultural milieu, was emerging into a new creature: *Homo Americanus*.

In 5000 B.C. this American did not much differ in his cultural accomplishments from primitive man elsewhere. At the time man in the Nile Valley was cultivating millet and barley and laying down the agricultural base upon which Egyptian civilization was to flower, the "American" was selecting the wild plants which would become his maize, potatoes, tomatoes, beans, and squash, on which he, too, would build his civilization.

In only one respect—and this is an important one for American cultural history—did he differ from the Eurasian. There was no Metal Age: man here never quit his Neolithic horizon, and his tool, although he did invent soft bronze, remained the tool of the *pithecanthropi*, the stone celt.

By the time the Egyptians had reached their cultural apogee and erected the Temple of Amon in 2100 B.C., the Babylonian civilization had come and gone; the legendary Cadmus had left the legacy of the alphabet, and the glory that was to be Greece was still contained in societies of Hellenic men abysmally primitive.

In America by that time, the period of great wandering had come to an end; vast spaces of the American earth were men-filled. Out of these cysts of geography cultures came into being. In the hyperborean regions, the Eskimo, flat of face and rotund of body, still lived in the environments of the Ice Age; on the North American plains, tall, keen-eyed tepee dwellers regulated their lives to the biology of the roving animal; farther south, where the caress of the sun was longer, the Indian, becoming partly sedentary, cultivated his plants and under the shelter of rock eaves erected crudely constructed pueblos. At the other extreme of America, the antipodal south, giant Fuegians, their naked bodies wrapped in guanaco skins, walked the frozen tundra, leaving the imprint of their widely spreading feet, "patagones," on the firebound land, Tierra del Fuego.

In the luxuriant jungles of that same South America, naked Indians with filed teeth hunted man and beast; while west of these dwelling places of the Amazon and the Orinoco was the evening land of the Andes. There in the high, cold, dun-colored valleys, a huge-lunged people were developing a great civilization. Around a frigid Andean lake called Titicaca, an Aymara-speaking race had, by the year 1000 B.C., laid down the agricultural patterns that would become Tiahuanaco, while around them and strewn over the rock-hard world there were many other tribes speaking Quechua, a related language. In time these "Incas" would form all the other Andean tribes into an empire. North of the Incas were the Quitus; north of the Quitus the territory of the Chibchas, whose strange custom of having their "king" wash off his gold-dust-smeared body in a mountain lake was to create the myth of El Dorado.

Between these geographic monsters, North and South America, lay Middle America and Mexico, their broken mountains studded with belching volcanoes. They were to be the scene of the great civilizations of ancient America.

Most of Mexico had a homogeneous culture. Whether it was Totonac, Toltec, Zapotec, Huastec, Maya, or Aztec, tribe was developed from family; animal diet was supplemented by crude agriculture—plots of ground were burned and seeds inserted in holes made by a fire-hardened stick. Agriculture revolved around corn as the staple, and society was then, as it has remained ever since, machineless. There were no draft animals; the denominator of speed was the foot. Dress was the breechclout; men walked on sandaled feet and women wore a short-petticoated cincture of woven cotton cloth; bare breasts matched bare feet.

In all these tribes society was organized on cognate kin-ship; the unit was the clan, and each clan had a totemic name. Together these clans became a tribe, bound not by the holding of land but by the ties of blood. Equally homo-geneous was their religion. Belief was animistic: everything in their world, animate or inanimate, possessed "soul," every-thing was alive, sentient, willful. Gods, both good and evil, had to be propitiated; and art, when it evolved, became ded-icated to the metaphysics of this theology. Stoneworking was universal among them. The tides of cultural inheritance ebbed back and forth among all tribes of Mexico and Middle America until that which had been the exclusive cultural property of one tribal kin became the cultural currency of all. There was no later cultural intrusion from either Europe or Asia—within itself and by itself, the Americas created their own world.

5. Pre-Aztec Cultures

THE TENOCHAS, called "Aztecs," were the last to arrive at the valley of Anáhuac.

In point of historical fact they were so late in becoming the overlords of Mexico that other greater civilizations had come and gone and were only vague memories in mythology. The sole reason that "Aztec" is so deeply ingrained in history and man's knowing is that it was the dominant political tribute state at the time of the Spanish conquest in 1519, even though its domination was only over a portion of central Mexico. However, when "Aztec" burst upon Europe, it was etched deep in human memory. Today's Mexico had then no generic name, and so the name of the island tribute state "Mexico" was imposed upon and over the whole of the land.

It was only much later when the Spanish priest-chroniclers began to question the Indians in regard to their origins and beliefs that they were made aware of the pre-existence of civilizations far, far older and far greater than the Aztecs.

Decades of patient archaeological search have now revealed, all in all, a good deal about these pre-Aztec cultures; with each year scholars are pushing back time. "The earth became our archive," wrote George Vaillant, "the shovel, our reading glass, and in that which nature has eternally destroyed—scattering our materials all over the land," [81] they found and are continuing to find this new archaeological evidence.

By 1000 B.C. the great migrations were over. Peoples filled the fertile lands and were beginning to build temple-cities. In central highland Mexico, throughout the hotlands of Vera Cruz, and in the highlands of Guatemala, they laid down their city centers. Man became sedentary; he had developed agriculture and he knew leisure. During the same period in the "other lands," the Phoenicians were devising the alphabet, the Greek-Dorians were arriving in the Peloponnesus, and Europe, thinly populated, was coming out of raw savagery.

One tribe was already evident: the Olmecs (800 B.C.–A.D. 600?), who lived in the hotlands of Vera Cruz and Tabasco; 800 B.C. marks the beginning of the preclassic period in Mexico.

It was long suspected that the Olmec would prove to be one of the earlier cultures and now radiocarbon dating from the Olmec site at La Venta has confirmed the evidence that Olmec structures "appear to have been constructed and used during . . . four centuries . . . 800–400 B.C." [26]

In Aztec mythohistory, the Olmecs were known as "the people who live in the direction of the rising sun" [15] and a glyph history of them shows that their paradisiacal "wealth" consisted of rubber, pitch, jade, chocolate, and bird feathers. We do not know what they called themselves. "Olmec" derives from *olli* (rubber); their symbol, often seen, is that of the tree of life, the "weeping wood." They traded rubber and they presumably made the rubber balls used for the game called *tlachtli*. A talented and mysterious people, they appeared as early as 1000 B.C. along the Isthmus of Tehuantepec (where the waist of Mexico is slender and level between the two oceans), but they were particularly centered about the Coatzacoalcos River basin on the Gulf Coast. For untold centuries burial mounds and pyramids built by them lay covered by the jungle; here archaeologists have found carved jade, sensitively modeled clay figurines "of an unprecedented high artistic quality," [24] said Miguel Covarrubias.

Only in recent times have the great Olmec stone heads been unearthed, by Dr. Matthew Stirling. At Tres Zapotes he found one colossal head, seven feet high, flat-nosed and sensually thick-lipped. The carving is sensitive and realistic; the style is found among no other people and once seen will never be forgotten or confused with any other. Other colossal heads have been found; in similar style there are carved masks, heads in smaller scale, and votive axes, all exhibiting the same squat figures with perforated noses, pronounced Mongoloid features, and narrow slits for eyes. These have been found in widely scattered areas. The Olmec large-scale monuments, however, are found mostly between Vera Cruz, Tabasco, highland Guatemala, and Oaxaca—this is definite Olmec land. A stela found at Tres Zapotes and numbered by the bar and dot system, bears what is by far the earliest recorded "American" date: 31 B.C.

Only now are Olmec structural complexes coming into focus. They had temple-cities, erected stone stelae to mark the flight of time or to commemorate important events; the stepped pyramid, the courtyard, the *tlachtli* ball game, were all cultural features in general use. The Olmecs still occupied their traditional tropic land when the Spanish first arrived. There is no record of them beyond the observation that they tattooed their bodies, inlaid their teeth with jade, flattened their heads, plucked their face hair, hunted heads for trophies, flaying the skin and tanning them as the Jivaros in the Upper Amazon did the tsantsas, the shrunken human head trophies.

The art of the Olmecs is unique—simple, direct, forceful. There is nothing quite like it in all Mexico. Yet aside from this "art" they must have been possessed of certain social

5. *Olmec culture, symbolized by the great stone heads with thick lips and broad nostrils, found in the hotlands of Vera Cruz and Tabasco. The Olmec culture dates back to and beyond* 800 B.C.

6. *Zapotec art, which centered about Monte Albán, is typified by this funeral ceramic.*

dynamics to stamp their pattern on Mexico's cultural history.

The Mayas (2000 B.C.–A.D. 1697), who appeared early, had a great influence over the development of culture in Mexico and were the longest-lived. For what length of time they built their temple-cities before their first calendar was set up is not known. The earliest stela, at Uaxactún, is dated A.D. 328.

From the earliest times there was much cultural interchange among all these peoples. A large trading area at Xicalango in Campeche was the Maya contact center for the outside world where, under terms of peace, things of their lands were exchanged with Central Mexico. Possessed of large and traditional tribal lands, the Mayas, free of any large-scale outside invasion until the twelfth century, perfected their calendar, glyph writing, and stone carving, and evolved the complex temple-cities which can still be seen today. Their influence on the other cultures in the high Mexican plateaus was very marked.

Monte Albán (500 B.C.–A.D. 1469), a ceremonial center and temple-city, lies in Oaxaca atop high treeless hills overlooking the valley and the present-day Spanish city of the same name. One of the oldest in Mexico, its occupation continued from the earliest preclassic period, perhaps as early as 1000 B.C., until the coming of the Spaniard in 1522. This immense time period of twenty-five hundred years is divided into five archaeological horizons. Its beginnings are shrouded in mystery. Dr. Alfonso Caso, who first uncovered it and has worked on its problems continuously for twenty years, believes that its formal structures date as far back as 500 B.C. Even as early as this they had already developed glyph writing, a calendar, and a complete cosmogony.

Who were the early builders? From the beginning it seems it was a city, although not habitable, of the gods, visited by men and women alike. Before the city (its original name is unknown) took on its Zapotec character, it had from the earliest times a temple with a frieze of dancing figures done in the Olmec style, a "powerful and mysterious archaism of expressive monsters." These Olmec-styled figures and stelae, with the still indecipherable glyphs, are the primary mystery of Monte Albán.

One will grasp how really early all this was if one remembers that in the same period of world history Nebuchadnezzar was destroying Jerusalem and carrying off the Jews to their first slavery; Cyrus, king of the Persians, was on the loose and the whole Middle East was in an expansion mood;

by the time the people of Mexico were beginning to set up their temple-city states, Xerxes had conquered Egypt and was setting off to invade Greece. Although the American man had none of the stimulation of the Fertile Crescent of the Near East—which brought the wheel, iron, and the alphabet to the world—he was advanced in city planning, writing, and sculpture.

At about A.D. 300 Monte Albán moved into a transition period, threw off its Maya influence, and turned to its own sources—the Zapotec. For the four hundred years that followed, the great plaza was enlarged, and temples, pyramids, ball courts, and the frescoed tombs were constructed.

The Mixtecs (668*–1521), whose capital city was Cholula (the present-day Puebla), occupied a geographical buffer zone between the coast and the highland; they were subject to all the recurring waves of conquest, first from the coast (Olmec), then from the highlands (Toltec). Later they became conquerors; after 1350 they extended south into Monte Albán, only in turn to be overrun by the Aztecs after 1450.

The Mixtecs have wondrous tales to tell of themselves. The Indian noble Ixtililoxochitl, writing in the seventeenth century, told of giants and Olmecs and much about the pyramid to the Plumed Serpent, the greatest in all the Americas.[44] Quetzalcoatl was a mysterious figure through all Mexico and Yucatán. That he once lived can be assumed (later rulers of the Toltec took his name as a patronymic just as Moslem rulers today carry the name of their prophet or the Romans called themselves "Caesar"). It is difficult to separate man from myth. Quetzalcoatl was a demiurge, priest, and ruler, conceived by virginal birth years after his father's death (his mother was made pregnant when she swallowed a piece of jade); he was ruler of the Toltecs for twent years. He lived in Tula, lost a civil war,† fled with a good-sized Toltec force, reached the Coatzacoalcos River on

---

* This date was reached by Covarrubias by dedi ing the five hundred years of Olmec occupation of Mixtec land, mentioned by Juan de Torquemada in his *Monarquia Indiana* (Madrid, 1723), from the date of 1168, when the Olmecs were driven from Cholula.

† What perhaps was a real political struggle for power between two concepts of government—the peace-loving "positive" Quetzalcoatl against the "negative" Tezcatlipoca, "Smoking Mirror," who brought the terror—was rationalized to "correlate historical events with an older mythus." [81]

7. *Mixtec art forms resemble the Aztec. Mixtec civilization, beginning as early as 700 B.C., was centered about Cholula. The illustration is taken from a part of a Mixtec codex, an origin myth.*

the day of 1-Reed in Aztec reckoning (the sign under which he was born), and set sail into the open sea with the prophecy that he would again return on the recurrence of that date.

He left his impress on the Mixtecs, who, like the others in this high cultural period, had writing and paper (some Mixtec codices survive). They were advanced in the arts of building and in agricultural and social planning, and, despite wars of rapine and conquest, their cultural influence lasted over thousands of years; they greatly influenced the Aztecs.

The Huastecs (500 B.C.–A.D. 1521), who occupied northern Vera Cruz and extended inland as well to include highland Mexico (now the states of Tamaulipas, San Luis Potosí, Hidalgo, and Querétaro), have also been determined to have been one of the earlier cultures,[9] enduring in more or less continued activity for two thousand years and silenced only by the arrival of the Spanish. The distinctive art forms of the Huastecs have been known for many decades, but it is only in the last fifteen years that Huastec architecture has been uncovered.[10]

The Totonacs, "discovered" by the collectors of modern art because of their nonobjective art styles, also appeared during the preclassic period. The Totonacs had, so far as it is known, an uninterrupted cultural continuity in central Vera Cruz from approximately 500 B.C. until the arrival in 1519 of Hernán Cortés. They formed a sort of linguistic "sandwich" between the Olmecs and the Huastecs, who were of Maya

8. *One of the Totonac "laughing heads."*

stock and speech. Totonac country has yielded for many decades some of the "finest and most sophisticated specimens of Indian art" [12]—the freehand clay figurines always in laughter; the "laughing heads" and life-sized stone heads attached to a tenon, meant to be placed in walls as an architectonic motif; the strange U-shaped objects as large as horse collars and resembling them in size and shape, carved from polished green or black stone, exquisitely decorated and made for an unknown purpose. This art, gay, sybaritic, a contrast to the austere Maya or Aztec form, is a Totonac characteristic. They also left behind an impressive number of temple-cities which, although covered by jungle and eroded by the centuries, still retain their form, so that Mexican archaeologists are able to restore them. All this culture which had been nurtured for a thousand years was at the disposal of the Aztecs.

9. *Totonac architecture is typified by the temple of Tajín at Papantla in Vera Cruz. The niches held small idols; the temple was atop the pyramid. The Totonacs began as far back as 500 B.C. They were a functional tribe in full flower when Cortés arrived in 1519.*

In the valley of Anáhuac, in the central Mexican plateau, after 200 B.C., the Toltecs learned better management of their agriculture and produced a social surplus. With that, Teotihuacán came into being.

Toltec-Teotihuacán (200 B.C.–A.D. 900), "Place of the Gods," thirty-two miles northeast of Mexico City, dwarfs in magnitude all else in Mexico and Middle America (save perhaps Tikal in Guatemala); the remains of the great ceremonial city alone cover an area of eight square miles. It challenges the imagination how the Toltecs at so early a period could have marshaled so many people—with enough leisure, unoccupied with their fight about the feeding trough —to build and maintain so enormous a religious center. So renowned was Teotihuacán that it served as model for all subsequent temple-cities, and the Toltecs remained—even when monuments were covered and were only a vague memory—the master builders, and thereafter all artisans

10. *Toltec-Teotihuacán was the classic culture of the valley of Mexico. It endured from 200 B.C. until A.D. 900. The symbol of Quetzalcoatl—a serpent's head wreathed in quetzal plumes —is Toltec.*

who were masters, especially painters and *tlacuilo* writers, were called "Toltec" even down into Aztec times.

The history of these Toltecs, less vague when read in the light of recent archaeological findings, is found in the *Annals of Cuauhtitlan;* later, less speculative literature [53] and further exploration and excavation have filled in the gaps. The Toltecs spun in cotton, which means that they maintained contact with the hotlands, as cotton does not grow in the high plateau; men had thicker garments for cold weather and women dressed in loose-fitting *huipilli* and wrap-around skirts; warriors wore (as did the Aztecs one thousand years later) quilted cotton armor; their weapons were like those of the Aztecs; and their priests, as did the Aztecs, went about filthily in unwashed black tunics that swept the ground. Their chiefs dressed as did the common man, only more elaborately, and they were monogamous. In their houses the Toltecs constructed the *temascal* steam bath, a common feature among the Aztecs.

When Toltec history emerges through the myths that surround it, it follows a pattern. A priest-astrologer guided them through Mexico until they found a fertile valley. There they built their city of Tollan or Tula. The choronology of their kings, which must have been chanted for centuries, was etched into the memory pattern, so that when repeated to a double-languaged scribe and set down in the sixteenth century, it gave the names of their rulers. It told of Toltec dominance under their eighth ruler, a rule which embraced all the land between Jalisco to the north and Cuernavaca to the south; it told of the elaborate ritual of their polytheistic religion and it mentioned in detail the woman known as *Xochitl* (pronounced "sho-chitl"), who made popular the beverage now called "pulque" by fermenting the juice of the maguey plant.

Like their rivals of the same period, the Toltecs of Teotihuacán had ideographic writing, tribal records, *amatl*-paper books which pictured their bewildering cosmogony; they also had the fifty-two-year cycle, magical *tonalpohualli* (the numeration of fate), a system of prognostication based on a period of 260-day count, and a lunar calendar for everyday use. And they built the awe-inspiring temple-city Teotihuacán.

Teotihuacán endured from 200 B.C., the approximate time of its shadowy and tenuous beginnings, until about A.D. 900. Its period of slow decline is revealed in its pottery. Here is reflected the gradual change that came over a tribe that lost its political power but kept its respect among others. Another tribe, the Chichimecs, moved into the Toltec domain and took up the remains of "empire" but found themselves swallowed up in the chaos between the years 1100 and 1300 that followed the breakup of the "age of cultural unity." [81] Meanwhile the Toltecs, now migratory, developed two other cultural areas, Tula and Xochicalco.

Tula (A.D. 900–1156) is of the greatest importance. Tula, which was once regarded as pure mythology—prompting an ironical remark by one writer about the "vague science of anthropology and the exact art of myth"—has been confirmed by archaeology. The very close resemblance of its architecture to the cities of Mayapán, principally Chichén Itzá in Yucatán, confirms the trek of the Toltecs to that region in the twelfth century. Is this Tula, the legendary "Tollan" as described by the padre-chronicler Sahagún, the beautiful city "of rich palaces of green jade and white and red shell, where the ears of corn and pumpkins reached the size of a man, where cotton grew in the plant in all colours and the air was always filled with rare birds of precious feathers . . ."? If Tula is Tollan, eight centuries have changed the land. It is now dry, parched, dust-filled, and no "precious bird" in its right avian mind would go there.

And yet the description of the city is not as mythical as first believed. Archaeologists found elaborately carved and painted walls, a stepped pyramid with the remains of a temple at its summit, with the symbol of Quetzalcoatl—two stone-painted serpents fifteen feet high acting as caryatids for the elaborate façades of the temple; carved pillars for the temple of the warriors; immense stone-carved figures; and that sculptural idea which traveled farthest, the reclining figure of Chac-Mool looking blankly into space and holding a stone tray on which palpitating human hearts were placed as food for the gods. This same frightening figure, without any change, was to be carved and set up in the capital of the Aztecs, and was to find its way eight hundred miles south into Yucatán.

Xochicalco (A.D. 700–1200), of Toltec origin or influence, with its famous temple to the Plumed Serpent, was built more or less at the same time as Tula (A.D. 900). Lying lonely in the sun on top of bare hills, not more than twenty direct miles south of Cuernavaca, it was one of the first "ruins" to enter literature, having been explored by Antonio Alzate in 1777 and illustrations of it published in 1810 by Alexander von Humboldt.

11. *Tula is Toltec. The fabulous city, north of Mexico, is presumed to have been built between* A.D. *900–1156 and ruled by Quetzalcoatl. Many Toltec architectural forms are found at Chichén Itzá in Yucatán.*

Xochicalco, "Place of Flowers," was a ceremonial, perhaps administrative, center for the tribes which lived in this region. It is situated on the highest hills, looks down upon two freshwater lakes two miles distant, fish-filled, with much game and a fertile country and in a strongly fortified position. The hills were artificially flattened and terraced with strong points for defense. Four roads coming from the four cardinal directions led into the principal plaza, where the temple to Quetzalcoatl stands. The Aztecs knew of it and were influenced by it.

All the cultures listed here—and there are many more—were established on Mexican soil as long as twenty-five hundred years before the Aztecs made their appearance as an organized tribe. By the time they put in their appearance close on to A.D. 1200, the tides of these earlier cultures had swept back and forth across the face of the land, devastating one another, at the same time developing all the varied aspects of much of that which we call civilization.

And to all this the Aztecs were the heirs.

II

The People

6. The Origins of the Aztecs

THE "AZTECS" came into Anáhuac, the valley of
Mexico, in A.D. 1168. This, recorded in their written
ideographic histories, has been synchronized with our calendar; no one has cast doubt on it.

The Tenocha-Aztecs were wanderers, a landless, "want-
ing" tribe who came out of the north of Mexico (some hold
from what is now southwestern United States but there is no
evidence of it); they were of Nahuatl speech, that language
which was also the speech of the Toltecs. The Aztecs were of
the "have-nots," moved about, settling here briefly, wandering there, nibbling at the nether edge of others' lands
until a battle ensued; then peregrination began all over again.
The date 1168, to be sure, does not tell us with certainty
that the Aztec settlement in Mexico began then, but only,
as Dr. Vaillant believed, that at that time the Aztecs, who
were then cultural nonentities, had begun to use a calendar
which had been in general use for a thousand years. Who
were the Aztecs and from whence is answered in their
mythohistories.* Like all other such origin myths, these
differ in detail, not in basic content. The Incas came out of
caves; Greeks were given divine guidance by an *autologos*
in a darkened sanctuary; Christian myths overflow with heavenly inspired grottoes. And so the Aztecs. They found in a
cave the Hummingbird Wizard, the famous Huitzilopochtli

---

* The word "Aztec" as applied to the Tenochas is not of certain origin. They said that they came from some fabled land,
Aztlan; because of this the Spaniards referred to them as "Aztec"; of a certainty they neither called themselves that nor were
they called that before the Conquest.

(a name the conquistadors never mastered, calling it *Huichilobos,* Witchy-wolves"). The idol gave them advice. It sounded well: wander, look for lands, avoid any large-scale fighting, send pioneers ahead, have them plant maize, when the harvest is ready, move up to it; keep me, Huitzilopochtli, always with you, carrying me like a banner, feed me on human hearts torn from the recently sacrificed. . . . All of which the Aztecs did.

The number, even approximate, of the Tenocha tribe at that time we do not know. It was minuscule—perhaps a thousand, perhaps five thousand, not much more. At least in so thickly settled an area as the valley of Anáhuac they were so insignificant that their arrival at the lakes passed completely unnoticed, and there is no record of their arrival in the stately forest of Chapultepec in the generation about A.D. 1250. All this is understandable. No one regarded as "historical" the internal events of other tribes. History was perpendicular, not horizontal; it had no cross references. During these "wandering years," the Aztecs were absorbing the culture of their neighbors. They grew. They made enemies. They expanded. Their clans being too small for wife-yield, they took to wife-stealing, and now for the first time their neighbors around the valley took cognizance. They were set upon. One part of the tribe was swept into servitude, another escaped to one of the swampy islets out in Lake Texcoco. Those left behind were involved in the wars of their captors, wherein they displayed such valor that when asked to name a boon, they asked for the daughter of the chieftain, so that through her they could form a respectable lineage. It was granted, but they sacrificed the beautiful girl, flayed her, and draped the skin over their head priest so that he might impersonate the Nature Goddess. When the chieftain of their captors, the father of the girl, arrived in gorgeous array, he expected, naturally, to attend a wedding ceremony. Instead he found—this. One can somehow understand his wrath. Those Tenochas who escaped the butchery by his warriors fled and joined their tribesmen on the second islet on the lake.

Tenochtitlán, the island city-state, began historically in 1325. The lakes wherein the incipient Aztec capital lay, as shapeless as free-swimming protoplasm, were five,* situated

* Contiguous but with five names: Chalco and Xochimilco were fresh-water; Texcoco, brackish; the most northern, Xalto-cán and Zumpango, very salty.

in the valley of Anáhuac, a level plain over 7,000 feet in altitude. From the high snow-covered mountains that surrounded it there poured the brawling streams that made these lakes, which were fifty miles long, five hundred square miles in surface, and ringed with tall, slender marsh grass. The lakes were deep in some places but shallow in others, especially about the islets that formed the city of the Tenochas. The exigencies of the moment called first for housing. Wattle and daub houses thatched with the marsh grass came first. Later in the same year, 4-Coatl (1325), the Tenochas dedicated their first temple. In the beginning, and by agreement with the tribes that ringed the shore, they had permission to use border lands for planting. This land they augmented with *chinampa* agriculture, a method in which outsized wickerwork oval-shaped baskets were made and then towed to their islets, anchored to the shallow bottom and filled with earth. In these they grew their crops. Mexico-Tenochtitlán thus was hand-fashioned.

During the years 1403–55 (Aztec III period) the growing city-state, through alliance and war, depressions and recovery, outgrew the primitive stage and filled in the background

12. *Aztec temples and houses, with a chieftain in march toward them. Footprints indicate migration or movement. Redrawn from an Aztec codex.*

with new and enlarged cultural horizons. Thereafter the Aztecs took the center of the Mexican stage and became the principal directors of life within and without the valley of Anáhuac. So they expanded as all peoples expand, as life itself lives, at the expense of other lives and of other peoples; this is reasonable, understandable, and natural.

Techniques moved slowly. Metalworking came up from South America by slow stages through indirect trade, arrived in Mexico about the eleventh century. Although advanced in many ways, these Americans were yet without the wheel, the rotary quern, and draft animals. Mexico in 1519, as C. A. Burland said, "was where Sumer and Egypt stood in 3500 B.C."; the picture, however, is not that clear.

At the same historical moment—A.D. 1100—that the Incas in Peru were emerging from a similarly obscure position to become a real empire,[15] the Aztecs were, by the same imperialistic means, evolving as the overlords of Mexico.

So, within these extreme dates of 1168–1521, the Tenochas, called "Aztecs," came into their own.

7. Appearance—What Manner of Men

T HE BASE of Aztec society was the plebe—the *macehualli*—the common Indian.

While his place was less that of an automaton than mere man under the Inca empire, where he was only a "head count," still he was, in labor terms, both rank and file. *Macehua* derived from "to suffer" or "to earn merits"—in reality he did both. He was a member of a clan and part of an earth cell, of a sort of mutual-aid society; he was, in summary, an able-bodied, taxpaying Indian. First and foremost he was a farmer, in European terms a peasant, and, in the still highly valid expressions of Oswald Spengler "the eternal man, independent of every culture . . . one who preceded it, . . . outlived it, a dumb creature propagating himself from generation to generation, limited to soil-bound callings and aptitudes, with a mystical, dry, shrewd understanding that sticks to practical matters."

Yet this common Aztec was something more. He was also a warrior, part of an agrarian militia. As the common Roman was a worker-soldier, so the common *macehualli* (plural: *macehualtin*) must be understood as a farmer-warrior.

Like most of the indigenes in Mexico, he was short—between 5 feet 1 and 5 feet 5—broad-headed and thickset. Tireless, he was used to walking since childhood and could carry a load of seventy-five pounds, fifteen hours a day. His arms were long and feet broad in proportion to his height; his gait straight and inclined to be pigeon-toed; the arches, as one can see in Aztec drawings of footsteps, were very high.

The head was characterized by the jet-black eyes, lidded with the epicanthic fold, which gives the eye an almond shape. The hair was dark, coarse, abundant, except on his body and face. He was relatively beardless, and face hair was deemed objectionable, so that mothers used tweezers to

13. *The Aztec warrior-farmer, called* macehualli. *As plebe he was the base of Aztec society. These figures, redrawn from the* Codex Mendoza, *show two aspects of his life—as farmer and as warrior.*

pluck it out and applied hot cloths to stifle the hair follicles. They were "beardless," even though Cortés said that the Tlascalans had "barbers to shave you." The Aztec face was further made prominent by a hooked Roman nose (although any citizen of that *imperium* would have been shocked at so odious a comparison) which grew more so in old age. Their color varied from dark to light brown; the face could assume a fierce mien and often great dignity, an expression they carried into battle or palaver.

Aztec women were naturally smaller (4 feet 8), and delicate. Yet it was a false frailty. They bore children quickly, often in the milpa fields; they followed their men on long marches (the women attached to the Mexican army in recent times were part of the quartermaster corps), and carried their share of the load, including the inevitable baby. Many of them were of striking appearance; the Spaniards thought so, married them and found them attractive. Doña Marina, "The Tongue," an Indian girl who helped talk the Spaniards into victory over Moctezuma, was declared to be an "excellent woman . . . full of grace."

Dress was, for the common man, simple and expedient; the same raiment was worn night and day. All wore the loincloth (*maxtli*), a cincture that was passed between the legs and brought about the waist, its two ends hanging in front and back and usually embellished. In this he worked on marches where he carried cargo. The mantle (*tilmantli*)— in today's usage, the manta—was a rectangular piece of woven cloth tied over one shoulder, made at first from the coarse fibers of the maguey (*metl*) and later, when contact with the hotlands was general, from cotton. They used neither buttons nor pins. When the *tilmantli* was sufficiently flowing, it covered the whole body when seated. Many of these often were beautifully woven; of this however we have little or no evidence except their own pictures and the descriptions by their conquerors. The common Indian mostly walked with naked feet until he grew in social importance; then he traveled in sandals (*cactli*) made from animal skin or maguey fibers. For the chieftain or demigod, they were of gold.

Hair styles had some variation: in everyday use the hair hung in bangs and was cut in back by barbers with an obsidian knife—*Pagankopf* the Germans would call it—or it

14. *Aspects of Aztec cookery. In the upper left,* camoti *(sweet potatoes); to the right is the stone* metatl *on which corn is ground. The woman cooks red peppers on a* cumal, *and in the lower righthand corner newly baked corncakes are covered to retain freshness.*

was allowed to grow long and braided into a thick pigtail. When at war it was decorated with two turkey or eagle feathers.

Woman's dress in this plebe class, while of only one cut, varied greatly in design, color, and pattern, for women were the principal weavers. The woman wore an underskirt (*cueitl*) of ankle length and often magnificently embroidered; when abroad she would put over this a poncholike dress (*huipil*), a rectangular piece of cloth with a slit through which the head passed, the sides sewn except for armholes—a prosaic description of some of the finest weaving in pattern and color found in the continent, which Bernal Díaz, then an impressionable young man of twenty-three, found "rich and beautifully ornamented." Her sandals, lighter than those used by men, she wore only on journeys or if her social position demanded it. Her hair, long and lustrous and black, grew to full length; it was braided with ribbons for festival days, allowed to hang when about the house; it was gathered and wrapped about the crown of the head when she worked in the fields. Cosmetics were used, mostly by those of the "directing classes" or courtesans (*auianime*) and even sometimes by women of the common sort when their souls were touched by things at the markets. Unguents, perfumes, and creams were available.

8. The Traffic of Speech

Nahuatl (pronounced "*nah-wah-t'l*") was the language of the Aztecs.

It was neither their invention, nor perfected by them, since it was spoken by the Toltecs, Chichimecs, and numerous other tribes. It became, however, the lingua franca of Mexico and Central America (just as Quechua was that of the Incas in Peru) because of the conquest by the Aztecs, the penetration of their merchants and trade. And when later reduced to Spanish orthography, a further extension of it was made by the Church, which used it and translated the Christian catechism and other religious manuals into it, thus enlarging its speaking arena.

Nahuatl is one of the eight families of Uto-Aztecan stock. More detailed studies have been made of it, especially of Aztec, than of "any other American linguistic family." [59] This has been mostly because of the late B. L. Whorf, who was, *en passant*, a nonprofessional. Nahuatl speech is related to some of the language phyla of the Southwest Indians (Pima, Shoshoni, Sonora), hence the belief among some that the Aztecs were a fighting breed out of this region. There are seven hundred languages in Mexico; Nahuatl, which was somewhat confined to the central plateau but expanded following the Aztec conquest, belongs to one of the five large phyla of Macro-Penutian speech. Studies of it are highly specialized and its students use technical terms among themselves and in their publications which are never used in normal communications. If a layman were to read the one on "The origin of the Aztec -*tl*"—a suffix which the reader will find often in these pages—he would be as bewildered as Alice in her Wonderland when she came upon the "smile without the cat."

Nahuatl is a living language. Thousands still speak it, there are books and musical records in it, some of Mexico's foremost scholars converse in it; it is very graphic and plastic, as will be seen when the Aztec natural plant classification is discussed (see Medicinal Plants, page 107). The language was as compounded as the Aztec ideographic writing and capable of expressing great feeling and poetry, and although the early Spaniards found the suffix -*tl* very bewildering, six-teenth-century savants who mastered the tongue found it clear and harmonious, with an extended vocabulary.

Although there is no space here for a discussion of Aztec grammar, it had all the traffic of language—what one writer has called "the table manners of speech." Our modern grammar did not begin much before the Reformation; before that there was a cheerful indifference to syntax and spelling. Therefore it is amazing to find any people so removed as were the American Indians from the web of Old World communications who developed so involved a speech and grammar. There were derivative words and fusion "arising from context and pronunciation without regard to meaning"; agglutination was the natural result. What additions the Aztec made to his inherited speech, Nahuatl, is not known, yet it must have been substantial because, as a result of their conquests, new things were pouring into their world and they had to have some fixed grammar to receive them, with flections of person and tense. One of the first books printed in Mexico (1555) was Motolinía's *Vocabulario*. Grammars, catechisms, translations of texts from ideographic Nahuatl into Spanish orthography, have followed century after century until now there is quite enough for a serious study on "Aztec Literature." [20]

The speech of the Aztec *macehualli* had the same earth-iness as the soil man's everywhere; practical and with care-less speech habits, he fashioned his speech out of that usage stemming from need which is the living morphology of any language. Ordinary men were careless about the meaning of an affix, of the flections of person, number, case, gender; but in the *calmecac* schools of Mexico-Tenochitlán, where good Nahuatl speech was taught, corrected, extended so that high-placed persons could speak properly to the gods or impress visiting chieftains, this traffic of speech was carefully studied. It must have been. Those informants who worked with the first Spaniards in setting it down *knew* the grammar of their speech. This example will suffice; when Sahagún in 1529 began to take down the remembered sagas of the Aztecs, this is how he gave it in Nahuatl, using his own orthography, about the sun, the principal god-year:

Tonatiuh [sun] quautlevanitl
xippilli, nteutl [god]
tone, tlaextia motonameyotia,
tontoqui, tetlati, tetkaati, teytoni, teixlileuh,
teixtlilo, teixcaputzo, teixtlecaleuh.

The sun, eagle, dart of fire,
Prince of the year, God
illuminates, makes things glow, lights them with
    its rays,
is warm, burns people, makes them perspire,
    turns dark the
countenance of people, blackens them, makes
    them black as smoke.[50]

One said much in Nahuatl with little. And while the language was by no means as far-flung geographically as Quechua in Peru, which spread for the same reasons—i.e., conquest from Chile to Colombia—the Aztec speech penetrated far enough—from Mexico down to Nicaragua.

9. The Clan—the Aztec Holding Corporation

ALL—OR ALMOST ALL—of early native American societies were democratic.

There was rank without class. The community, not the individual, owned the land, and most decisions were made by popular ballot, as, for example, by the American Plains Indians. Or done in the manner which Tacitus described in writing of how the Germans came to decisions in the depths of their forests: "When the mass is to decide they take their seats fully armed . . . silence is then demanded . . . such hearing is given to king or chief as age, rank, military distinction or eloquence can secure . . . if a proposal displeases them, the people roar out their dissent; if they approve, they clash their spears."

When once the Indian began to sustain himself wholly from agriculture, he became a member of a commune. This could be a clan or sib (kin, related by blood) as among the Plains Indians, replete with totem or badge (like a coat of arms that identified the group), or an *ayllu* among the Incas, or it could be a *calpulli* (from *calli,* "house") as it was among the Aztecs. Most of the idigenous American communes were based on this type of organization, a clan as an economic unit united by supernatural (i.e., blood) bonds.

An Indian was born into a clan or *calpulli.* A *calpulli* was a group of houses of extended families. This clan owned certain lands which it held communally. A married man was lent his piece of land directly from the clan. No one had title to the land he worked, he was allowed only the produce of it; if he died without issue or the land was neglected or he was "drummed out" of his clan, the piece reverted back to the holding corporation. So exact were some of these, that records were kept on *amatl* paper of the various land tracts along with a rebus drawing of the holder's

55

15. Chinampas, *the "floating gardens" agriculture of the Mexican lakes. Into immense reed baskets, the Aztec put earth, then planted trees, anchoring the "floating garden" with staves. Out ot these Mexico City grew.*

name. According to their records there were seven original *calpulli;* once they settled on their island state, Tenochtitlán, these were enlarged into twenty.

Each of the clans owned, or held by treaty, land on the mainland. At first agricultural land was very limited; when a *calpulli* had none, its members industriously made *chinampas,* the so-called "floating gardens." These were the reed-woven baskets, eight feet in diameter, filled with earth and anchored in the shallow waters. Roots penetrating the basket bottom eventually firmly fixed them to the lake bottom. By this laborious method, a *calpulli* could enlarge its production and extend its clan holdings. Yet as their war conquests proceeded and more alien tribes were forced to yield terrain on the mainland, land grew plentiful and was divided proportionately among all the clans that formed the Aztec tribe. This system of land tenure was, as V. Gordon Childe calls it, "the fatal limitation of . . . Neolithic economy . . . the sole outlet for an expanding population was to annex more land for cultivation and suitable land was not unlimited." [16]

16. *The leaders of the Aztecs, heads of four clans (with their symbols above their heads), make their way toward the valley of Mexico in A.D. 1168.*

The Aztec clan system was not as rigid as the Peruvian system of the *ayllu*, which was overorganized. Yet it was so arranged that the whole group-family, the *calpulli*, moved as a social unit. "Mexican society," observed Dr. Vaillant, "existed for the benefit of the tribe and each member was supposed to do his part in preserving the community."

An Indian born into a clan could not lose his clan rights nor his right to a piece of clan-held land of a size sufficient to feed the numbers in his family; no one except the duly elected clan chieftains could force an Indian to forfeit these rights by expulsion for crime or other antisocial acts.

10. Marriage—the Tying of the *Tilmantli*

T IED TOGETHER—"spliced," in the Menckenian American colloquial—was not merely a figure of speech in Aztec society. Marriage was symbolized by the actual tying together of the edges of the *tilmantli* cloaks of bride and groom, and once so joined, they were supposed to be "hitched" for life.

A man married at twenty, a girl at about sixteen. In this society there was not a prohibition against bachelors as there was among the Incas. But economic factors and especially the preparation of food made it impossible for a man to live without a woman—corncakes, the irreplaceable staff of life, made twice daily, took two hours for each preparation and this was a woman's task.

Marriage was permitted only between members of different clans, for since all clan members were considered to be of the same blood, to marry within it would be incestuous. Since marriage was exogamous, it had a formality more complex than ours. A young man who contemplated marriage had to consult with the clan council. While sexual attraction and affection played a part, they knew then as now that one does not only marry the woman, one also marries the family. In this case it was more than a family contract, it was a social contract, for by it one's child inherited the birthright of entrance into a clan.

Old women were the marriage brokers. There exists a curious ideographic picture history, a sort of comic-book history, of the whole proceedings in the *Codex Mendoza*. While love was doubtless a determinant in courtship, it was not strongly emphasized. There were too many taboos. Remy de Gourmont felt that one must associate the idea of pleasure with the idea of love if one wants to understand anything of the movement of life. Yet it is also true that there is not in the Aztec pantheon a goddess of love, nor are there drawings or pottery showing acts of generation such as exist in Peru.

On the night of marriage the bride was carried to the groom's house on the back of the old woman matchmaker. All the principal members of the family involved as well as the headmen of the clan sat on mats facing one another and listened or dozed over the longwinded homilies—"here we are present . . ."—and between the periods of discourse a servant would pour out generous portions of intoxicating *octli*. This was more than marriage: clan was involving itself with clan; new blood was being brought into the family holding corporation.

Once the torrents of speech ended, then, in an effort to thwart the supernatural forces that surround this new life adventure, the man and girl seated on their grass mat had the knot tied, and they were united.

There was no fixed rule as to whether the man went to live with the woman's clan or she moved to his. Of a certainty the man did not partake of his bride during the first nights; these rites of the first nights, always referred to in

17. *Marriage—the tying of the* tilmantli. *An illustration from the* Codex Mendoza *depicts Aztec marriage customs. A man and woman, tied together, listen to homilies delivered by the old women who were the marriage brokers.*

anthropology as *jus primae noctis*, were enjoyed by the uncles, brothers, and even father of the bride. This was not regarded as incest but was done to save them both from what Lévy-Bruhl called the "mysterious miasma of marriage"—the males, the "group-friends" of the bride and groom, taking on this "responsibility" in order to spare the newly married any contact with the forces of the supernatural. If one's Italian can encompass the libretto of Mozart's *Marriage of Figaro*, this is the underlying theme of the opera: the Count wishes to impose his ancient prerogative of being the first to sleep with the bride.

The Aztec woman had rights, although they were not as far-reaching as the male's. Thus she could own property in her name, go to the council for justice, and if she was cruelly treated she could obtain a divorce. If divorced, she could marry again; if widowed, she could only marry within the clan of the deceased husband. Sterility was the great onus, the one thing a woman feared, for if she bore no children her man could peremptorily divorce her. To a people so involved in wars and death, children were important and necessary.

Then as now woman's power was based on sex; she controlled mostly by her organism; she was given the privileges which men concede when they are intoxicated by the fumes of desire. Then as now, woman was supposed to be chaste; she could be executed for adultery. Woman was not supposed to have extramarital affairs; a man could, however, provided it was with a married woman. If a married woman was involved in multiple coition and became with child she was not so much a problem as an unmarried one.

Woman naturally did not have all the opportunities afforded to man. Nor did she have, as among the Incas, the opportunity, if she was comely, of being brought out of the remotest regions to Cuzco, there to be precipitated into fame as a *Ñusta,* a "Chosen Woman." The Aztec woman had to rise on her own merit, or body, and even when influential her moves had to be made obliquely like the bishop's on a chessboard. By mere chance, she might be at some strategic spot at an opportune moment and so become the "tongue" in history, as in the case of Doña Marina, who was first sold into another tribe by her mother, who had remarried and did not want her presence about her new young husband. But in general she had her place. A woman might escape it as an individual, but she was drawn back to it as a species. And for good reason. The sole aim of the couple in this or in any other society was to free the female from all that was not purely sexual so that she could produce children. "Like generation," wrote Remy de Gourmont, "mother love is a commandment, a second condition for the perpetuity of life. . . ."

Concubinage existed in Aztec life. This is a paradoxical condition in a semiwelfare state. The Soviets insist that in theirs prostitution could not exist—it does. Theoretically, in so organized a society as the Aztec, prostitution was not supposed to be. Yet the great warriors of the Aztecs had their concubines; Moctezuma had "many women as mistresses," writes Bernal Díaz, who saw them. As always, the permanence of war brought much change in the traditional mores of the tribe. Armed conflict, as it does everywhere, loosened the ties of home and parental authority. Moral codes, essentially unstable, are at best only a handbook on the ideals of human happiness. "Morality," Remy de Gourmont has said, "will modify itself according to the mobility of the ideal." We have no precise idea how widespread this concubinage really was, but the Aztecs had a word for it: *auianime*.

11. *Calli:* The House

ONCE MARRIED, the couple built their own house.
Like all else it was a communal affair. This was
as true within Mexico-Tenochtitlán as it was without. The
type of house the *macehualli* built depended on where he
was and what he was. Finished, it reflected the "eternal
man," the peasant-tribesman. Even the greatest Aztec temples and palaces had their origin in the simple native house.
The Mayas knew this and immortalized such a peasant
house as an element in the decoration of the south wing of
the Nunnery Quadrangle at Uxmal. Dr. Vaillant confirms
that "the great cities of the Aztec had their origin in the
simple villages of sedentary tribesmen. . . . These were huts
with thatched roofs resting on walls of wattles smeared with
mud . . ." On the mainland, in the temperate zone of Anáhuac Valley, such houses persist to this day.

Within the "city" in a clan division, this house might be
of adobe, sealed with adobe "cement" and painted. We know
little about it—all has been destroyed. There is nothing left
here as there was at Machu Picchu or Ollantaytambo in
Peru, where one can follow the evolution of the *cancha* type
of native house into the complexity of the Inca palace. In
Mexico and in the Maya country there remain only the temples, pyramids, ceremonial ball courts; the link of evolution
between peasant house and florid temple has dissolved.

The interior was partitioned between kitchen and sleep-
ing-living portions. This can be clearly seen in the fragment
of Aztec codex that gives the genealogy of the *tlatoani,* hereditary chiefs of Azcapotzalco, with its illustration of a
typical Aztec house compound. At one end the fire and
kitchen—not a fireplace as we understand it, but rocks of
uniform height sunk into the beaten mud floor which merely
contained the wood. There was no chimney, no window, no
fireplace; the smoke found its own egress through the in-
terstices of the grass thatch. The fire was banked at night

and blown into life in the morning by the huff and puff of
the women.

Because the city grew out of "floating gardens" it had as
many canals as Venice, and usually a house of the common
man in the city fronted on a canal. The greater number of
houses, wrote Cortés, "were one story only." The materials,
according to the importance of the buildings, "were *tezontli*
[a volcanic stone easily worked, dull red in color] and adobes
that formed the walls plastered with lime, and in the suburbs

18. *An Aztec kitchen. At the left, the woman grinds the corn.
At the right, the woman shapes the corncake,* tlaxcalli. *In the
center is the* cumal, *on which the corncake is baked.*

and shores of the island [the houses were constructed] of
reeds and straw, appropriate . . . for the lower classes."
Many had gardens in which flowers or medicinal herbs grew.
By the house wall each had its own steam bath or *temascal*.

The corncakes were baked in the kitchen on a flat ceramic
dish (*cumal*); about were three-legged pots for boiling and a
variety of wooden spoons and other simple instruments for
cooking. In the other section of the house there was a raised
platform of earth on which a grass mat (*petlatl*) was spread.
The highest chieftain in the land had nothing better. This
surprised even Bernal Díaz, who wrote that they had "beds
of matting with canopies above, and no better bed is given,

19. *The temascal (steam bath). Most of the Aztec houses had them. Steam was produced by throwing water over heated stones or a wood fire.*

however great the chief may be . . ." The floor was stamped
earth; on it a *petlatl* or deerskin; windlowless, the grass-
thatched roofs were gabled or hipped. There were no doors;
only a cloth hanging in front of the opening kept out the
night cold. Clothes hung on pegs driven into walls. Paddles
for canoes, weapons, shields with the totemic device of the
clan were usually kept at the temple of the clan, and such
personal treasures as the family possessed—jade, feathers,
turquoise, festive clothes—were kept in a grass-mat chest,
called *petlacalli* (literally "house chest," a word which for
the Aztec was synonymous with "treasure"). There were no
tables, few used chairs; there were braziers (see Pottery and
Pottery Makers, page 85) to keep off the night chill, and for
illumination long slivers of pine wood, heavy with pitch,
which gave flickering light. Such, with variations depending
on rank, were the houses of the common Indian.

12. The Rhythm of Day and Night

"**I** MUST ACT because I live" were the first words of
the homunculus as he issued full-blown from the
alembic of Faust.

Man must live. Before day's break the Aztecs throbbed to
life with the beat of the wooden-tongued drums from the
great temples, as each of the smaller *teocalli* throughout the
city took its cue from the largest. As Venus, the morning
star, appeared to them at about 4 A.M., day was born and
the shell trumpets blown by the priests added to the din as
all other temples responded in counterpoint. Fires that had
been banked were blown to life and all over the city of Mexico-Tenochtitlán the pale smoke arose to a windless sky.

The Indian, as farmers do everywhere, rose at this hour
before the sun; city or land, the instinct was general. He
went to the steam bath, tossed water on the heated rocks,
passed through the vapor, dipped into the canal—rich man,
poor man, little man, chief, all responded in like manner to
the rhythm of Aztec life. Even Moctezuma rose at the same
time and went off to the courts to attend the dawn session.

All had morning ablutions. Aztec people were relatively
clean since water was available. The Spaniards were unable
to hide their surprise over this, coming from a Europe where
it was rare to bathe monthly. Andres de Tapia, a companion
of Cortés, affirmed: "Moctezuma bathed twice the day . . .
and all [of the Indians] bathed frequently." Since there were
no pigs and no fat, the Aztecs had no soap as we know it,
but they had a natural detergent, the roots of the *copal-
xocotl,* which the practical-minded Spaniard called the "soap
tree" (*Saponaria*); it made a lather and performed the work
of soap.

People newly married or too poor to have a slave (*tlacotli*),
or too lately wed to have children help them, had to prepare
the corn mass for the tortillas (*tlaxcalli*) twice daily themselves. There were no short cuts. Dry corn was steeped in

lime, then boiled and the corn skin pried loose; then it was brayed on the stone *metatl* with a grooved stone roller. This technique of corn preparation is so old that these artifacts appear among the first (as well as the last) archaeological objects to be found in the yielding earth. The unleavened cornbread, pancake-shaped, was baked on a flat *cumal*. This was the unvarying base food of their lives. In addition there were beans, chili pepper, fish, sometimes meat; maize could be made into tamales or *atolli*, a gruel made of maize flavored with honey and chili pepper. The culinary day began and ended with the same food. There were no cattle, goats, pigs, horses until white men brought them, thus no milk or cheese. There was nothing in all Mexico such as the maté used in Paraguay. Chocolate (cacao bean) was imported from the hotlands and only the well-provided had it. There was no grease for frying—everything was baked or boiled. Food was washed down with the mild intoxicant *octli*.

Corn was the base of life. All the tribes from Nicaragua to Arizona predicated their lives on it; all the temple-cities reared their economy on it. One's day began and ended with corn, and no matter how exotic were the foods of the Aztec leaders—which so surprised their conquerors—the base remained the simple corncake. No other plant has played so large a role in the development of cultures.

After this repast in semidarkness, man and woman put food and drink into a basket slung from the neck and went into the fields. If they worked in *chinampas,* these were cultivated; it they had fields assigned to them by the clan on the mainland, they poled their dugout to the fields, which they worked alone or collectively with other clan members. However, the high frequency of Aztec conquest and the need to put down rebellions among those newly or anciently conquered made any able-bodied man subject to instant war call. Such was the life of the farmer-warrior.

At night before dusk they were home again and once more there was the business of making corncakes. There were available in the market turkey, duck, deer, beans, squash, *camoti,* and such like; the evening meal, the largest, took place between four and five o'clock. The man or men squatted on the reed mats, helping themselves with their fingers from the pots of food brought to them. Women ate apart.

At night the room was lighted by pine splinters. By this light the women spun or worked their loom or prepared the pulque intoxicant; the men made paddles for canoes, grass mats, split their knives, arrowheads, and fish needles from obsidian, or chipped out stone querns; these they would trade in the market. When children began to make their yearly appearance, they were first placed in a cradle, and then as soon as they could move they became a part of this fabric of life.

Above all—children.

In this state, where war was perpetual and death constant, a rising birthrate, even though it meant the overpopulation of the city, was one of the important duties of all. As soon as the woman was pregnant, she was put under the protection of the god Tezcatlipoca. There is a whole pictured history in the *Codex Mendoza* of the birth, naming, rearing, discipline of a child, of the details of swaddling and the type of cradle. When the child was born, a magician (*tonalpoulqui*) was brought in by the parents from their own local clan temple. He consulted a horoscope (*tonalamatl*), a sort of book of fate, which was unrolled to its twenty-foot length. This was to determine if the child had been born under good or bad auguries. The naming was important, and if they found that the day was unlucky, the naming was put off till a better moment—the avoidance of misfortune itself is the enjoyment of positive good. "What's in a name?" To the Indians, everything. It is a badge, a "handle" (in the colloquial of midwestern United States). Many primitives have

20. *Life began and ended with the reading of the horoscope. At birth, old men consulted the* tonalamatl *(horoscope) for the lucky and unlucky days in a newborn baby's life.*

two names, social and personal. The personal was known and used only by the immediate family in the belief that if used too often, it might lose its power. In times of illness, the witch doctor used the real name to call the dying back to life. Boys were called after their fathers or grandfathers, usually dynamic names, as "Smoking Crest" (*Chimalpopoca*), "Obsidian Serpent" (*Itzcoatl*), "Speaking Eagle" (*Quauhtlatoa*); girls, who seem always to evoke a sense of poetry, were named after flowers, stars, birds, as "Ibis" (*Atototl*), "Green Flower" (*Matlal-xochitl*), or "Rain Flower" (*Quiauh-xochitl*).[74]

Since there was rank without class, it was not necessary to remain in a lowly state, even if one were born into it. In Peru the state existed for the Inca as a whole; among the Aztecs the state developed for the good of the individual. A man, as Dr. Vaillant pointed out, "could attain *rank* through his own efforts," but this rank his children did not automatically inherit "unless they earned it through equivalent tribal service." This could be accomplished in various ways—as a good farmer, hunter, artisan or soldier, or even merchant; excelling in any of these brought leadership.

Schooling of a sort was given at the clan's house for boys (*telpochcalli*). Each clan maintained a number of these under the administration of a master (*telpochtlatoque*). In charge was either a well-known warrior or an elder; here boys learned their own mytho-histories, rituals, and, above all, the use of war weapons. No doubt the master was soon able to ferret out those who showed dexterity with weapons—there was a small cadre of professional soldiers—and the young Aztec might be made to incline in that direction. Artisans and painters were revered too, or the boy might become a merchant, except that there was a tendency for this calling to go direct from father to son; or if he showed mystical leanings, he might be sent to the *calmecac* (which the Spaniards likened to a monastery), there to learn the intricacies of priesthood. In the expanding world of the Aztecs much was possible.

On the whole, training of the child remained in the parents' hands. Learning was by mimicry. One can follow the manner of this training in the recorded picture history. At three years of age, the child is allowed one-half tortilla per day—the tortilla being a foot in diameter; at thirteen he is eating two such outsized tortillas per day. The boy mimics the father; at first he carries a small bag suspended from his neck, for he must be his own draft animal; this is increased monthly until, like his father, he can carry sixty pounds. He fishes, plants, makes dugout canoes; he gathers rushes, weaves *petlatli,* makes sandals, carries, walks, runs. All of this is recorded in detail with word and picture.

Punishment was not always proportionate to the wrongdoing; certainly Aztec child discipline would not be approved by our overly timid society, which has created the "progressive child." For some infractions the father held the child's head over smoke; for others he was hand-pricked with a maguey thorn until the blood flowed. Since in these pictures the father is seen talking the while, admonishing while he is punishing (one sees by the speech scroll in front of his face that he is talking), the boy is being trained. This certainly was no worse than the fate Benvenuto Cellini suffered at the age of five when he thought he saw a lizard sitting on the coals of a fire: "My father . . . becoming instantly aware of what the thing was . . . gave me a great box in the ears which caused me to weep and howl with all my might." Cellini was pacified by his father's saying: "My dear little boy, I am not striking you for any wrong . . . but only that you remember that . . . you saw a salamander."

Daughters were like their mothers; dress was identical. At six the young girl is learning to spin; at eight she is sweeping the floors and eating one and a half tortillas per day; at thirteen she is making the tortillas, as she will do twice daily all the rest of her life.

This sense of dedication was the origin of Aztec social behavior. It was based on ancient mores dictated by custom, continued by custom and the authority of the parent. What was done is done; what was not, is not. Above all, their virtue was as the ancient Roman knew the word. The orientation of the Roman mind was as farmer-soldier, and although removed by time and distance, what has been said of Roman virtue in the farmer-soldier could be repeated for the Aztecs: "Unremitting work is the lot of the farmer, for the seasons wait for no man . . . accidents of weather and pest may frustrate him; he must accept compromise and be patient . . . routine is the order of his life . . . the life of the fields is his life . . . to him the knowledge born of experience is worth more than speculative theory. His virtues are honesty and thrift, forethought and patience, work and endurance and courage, self-reliance, simplicity and humility in the face of what is greater than himself."[4]

13. The *Milpa* Fields

Aztec life revolved around the *milpa*—the corn-field. And for good reason. No other civilization that has left its footsteps on the road of time has been predicated on the use of a single plant such as Indian corn (*centli*). Earlier than 3000 B.C., the cultures of the Middle East—Assyrian, Sumerian, Egyptian—were cultivating such leguminous plants as pulses, peas, lentils, vetches, whose high protein content made storage easy in semidesert lands. As for cereals such as wheat, "that most important extratropical grain," * it had been cultivated in India since Mesolithic times.[96] "Wheat . . . barley, rye, millet, panic-grass" were all part of the diet and economy of all who flourished in the Fertile Crescent. Yet none of these aforementioned civilizations depended solely on one plant as did those of Mexico and Yucatán.

The Egyptians, to give one pertinent example, according to the Papyrus Harris (Dynasty XX, *c*. 1200 B.C.) knew over thirty types of bread—the Aztecs had one. The Egyptians' diet was varied: peas, lentils, watermelons, artichokes, lettuce, endive, radishes, onions, garlic, leeks. They had fats, both vegetable and animal—the Aztecs had none. They had beef, honey, dates, as well as milk and cheese and even butter, which was unknown to the Aztecs until A.D. 1525. The stomach led in this refusal of man to accept his environment as fixed—it is from the kitchen that so many technical operations have sprung, e.g., furnaces, ovens, preservation, fermentation, grinding techniques. Independent inventions in the kitchen can be easily discerned by comparing the Egyptian women making unleavened bread, as shown in the drawings on the wall at Thebes circa 1900 B.C., with the Aztec method of making corncakes in A.D. 1520.

Corn made settled life possible in Mexico. Since these

---

* Emmer, an early wheat, has been found in Troy II (2300 B.C.).

people had but one such grain, it is understandable why it
played so great a part in ritual and in practice. The origin
of this grain is enveloped in botanical controversy. Although
some geneticists believe that the greatest diversity of varieties
comes out of Mexico, this is disputed. Paraguay is suggested
as the point of dissemination by some, challenged by others.
For the moment, "present evidence points to a dissemination
in all directions of the early forms from an unknown center.[71] In the beginning of the twentieth century, it was easy

21. *Egyptians making bread; from a mural at Thebes dated
1900 B.C. The meal is ground on a stone mortar, and the unleavened bread is baked on a flat oven. The baked bread is illustrated by the two circles.*

to state that maize—(the Awarak-Carib name for corn)—
developed out of *teosinte,* which was considered by most to
be the ancestor of corn much as wild grass was the ancestor
of wheat. Today the botanical applecart has been upset by
findings that point to a hybrid between a species of tripsacum
and maize as the original corn, (both *teosinte* and tripsacum
will cross with maize); and one of our great geographers
who is not easily stampeded into accepting the idea of Asiatic
contacts has stated—to make it still more complex—that
the origin of maize "cannot even now be attributed with
certainty to the New World as long as certain matters con-
cerning Southeastern Asia remain unsolved." [71] Whatever the
distribution centers, well-developed corncobs two inches in
length have been found in graves on the desert coast of Peru,

radiocarbon-dated 2500 B.C. Since one must begin at the beginning as Alice did in her Wonderland, we can begin at that date and allow those who wish to follow the maze of maize to pursue it. The starting point is in the bibliography.

Milpa culture has remained unchanged for three thousand years. What is true of Aztec farming technique is true of all others in this milieu. Milpas were located two to fifteen miles from the dwellings. If the land was forested, trees were ringed a year before and felled with ax-shaped stone celts. The bush and trees being burned, the ash was turned into the soil; larger trees were allowed to rot with time and provide humus. The earth was turned over and prepared by means of a digging stick (*coacoa*). March was the planting time. Corn kernels were place in holes four to five inches deep; in temperate zones beans and squash were put in at the same time; corn, growing faster, acted as host plant for the vines. April brought rain, and if the desired rain was withheld by

22. *An Aztec girl being instructed by her mother in the art of making corncakes. She grinds on a stone mortar. The circle in front represents the baking device, the* cumal. *On the wall are the baked cakes. From the* Codex Mendoza.

the gods, sacrifice was made to Tlaloc, the rain god. Of the eighteen months of the Aztec year, almost every one had its ceremonies and dances connected with the growing and harvesting of corn. The corn ripened in July and there was a feast for the Goddess of Young Corn (see The Festival Days, page 91). In August the rain which had been petitioned in April had to be held back; the Aztec somehow had to cajole the gods not to send rain which would spoil the harvest. So, another sacrifice, this time to a mature woman representing the Goddess of Ripe Corn.

What did all this yield the Indian in food? The studies made among the Mayas can apply approximately to the Aztecs, even though Maya agriculture in the hotlands had slightly more yield.[61] An acre gave twenty bushels of husked corn, a bushel being fifty-six pounds, which, fortuitously, coincides with a "cargo," of what a man could carry on his back. The average size of a milpa in Yucatán was ten acres; it would have been slightly less in the land-hungry Aztec territory. This gave an Aztec family a yield of two hundred bushels of corn yearly, or 11,200 pounds. To fell, plant, weed, and harvest this land with the aid of his wife and, say, four half-grown children, the Aztec farmer would have to expend about two hundred days. In the same field he would also plant beans, squash, pumpkins, adding to the yield of the field and also to be included in the produce of these two hundred days. Now since the average consumption of corn for tortillas is one and a half pounds a person a day, the family consumed only one third of what it produced, or 3,380 pounds' consumption a year as against 11,200 of yield, allowing a surplus for barter, trade, work taxes, and religious taxes. With a surplus of 165 unused days unless he was called to battle, the Aztec could use these in his particular craft, making grass mats, fiber sandals, canoes, weapons, etc. These he bartered for needed things at the markets.

Corn was the "basic." What else? Beans (etl) were grown in the same milpa, using the cornstalks for support, and squash and pumpkins, all of the genus Cucurbita, as well as the crooked-necked variety (ayote) were planted in between.

The Aztecs never had the other "basic," the potato, which nourished half of prehistoric South America; as a cultivated plant it was unknown throughout Mexico until it was brought to them by the Spanish. It first was carried to Spain, then it appeared in Europe as an article of diet for the poorer man, being introduced into England by Sir John Hawkins in 1565; then it returned to America. In Mexico it appeared "as an item of European diet," and in present-day Mexico, the potato is grown only for sale to those of a higher social position. Moreover, the potato was nowhere cultivated in Mexico or North America until after the Conquest. This is curious because wild tuber-bearing *solanums* are found as far north as Colorado. When the potato arrived, the Aztecs did not even have a name for it; they called it *pelon-camoti,* "the Peruvian sweet potato." As will be seen *there was never any direct communication between Peru and Mexico* until the white man appeared.[6]

The Aztecs had the sweet potato (*camoti*); it grew in the warmer valleys below 6,000 feet. An *ipomea,* a tuber-bearing morning glory, it is one of a great family of over one hundred species found throughout the world. The Chinese had the yam, which is Old World in origin; they called it *shu.* This yam, which is a *Dioscorea,* is found throughout Polynesia extending down to New Zealand, where it was assiduously cultivated by the Maoris. But one cannot botanically equate the *camoti* with the yam; they are different plants, though they are constantly confused with one another in the United States. Few Europeans are acquainted with one or the other so that when Thor Heyerdahl, the Wrong-Way Corrigan of anthropology, wrote didactically that "Tiki brought . . . in the fifth century the Peruvian sweet potato to New Zealand," it is the apogee of botanical ignorance.

The Aztecs developed, if not all the plants, then the names of much which is common on our table today: tomatoes (*tomatl*) grew below the frost line, planted in dormant milpas; the biting hot peppers (*chilli*), all varieties of capsicum, grew beside the *tomatl,* the gelantinous weeds valued as food for infants and the sick; various amaranth pigweeds, which they called *huautli,* were cultivated and made into flat cakes. Pineapples, which originated in the warmer areas from Panama to Brazil, reached Mexico probably from the West Indies and were grown as far north as Jalisco, appearing as high as 6,000 feet altitude. When they could, the Aztecs cultivated them. The very observant Jesuit traveler José de Acosta tasted them in Mexico in 1565 and found them "very coole, full of liquor and of easie digestion and in time of heate, fit to refresh." Cortés sent one to Spain "to our Emperor *Charles* which must have cost much paine and care to bring it so far . . . yet he did not trie the taste." [1]

Avocados—the Mexican word *ahuacatl* evolved into *ahuacate,* avocado—were grown in the warmer valleys of Aztec territory. The chewing-gum tree *chicle-zapotl* has come directly down to us in name and product. Chocolate (*chocolatl*), the beverage and the word, came to us from the Mexican farmer who cultivated the tree when his lands reached the lower, warmer areas; it thrived on the Pacific side as far north as Tepic. Everywhere chocolate appeared as an important element in native culture. It was an Aztec passion, sweetened with wild honey, perfumed with vanilla, tinctured with *achiotl*. Moctezuma quaffed it from pure gold cups: "a certaine drink made from cacao . . . served . . . with great reverence." [25]

The preparation and working of the milpa cornfield was collective. Members of the clan assisted one another, and when a farmer-warrior was away to the wars, his fields were cultivated by others of his clan. While the number of plants under cultivation seems impressive, agriculture was not as advanced as among the Incas. They did not prepare elaborate

23. *Aztec cornbins in which the harvested grain was kept. At the right, one woman stores corn grains in a large ceramic urn, another woman holds the* tamale, *still a popular food after three thousand years.*

terracing as was done in the Andes; they were not soil-makers, except in the expedient of the *chinampas*. They had no fertilizer other than their own feces, where the Incas had bird guano and llama offal. Irrigation was casually developed because of the nature of the land; the run-off of the rain could not be harnessed as was done in Peru. Irrigation techniques, which are inseparable from a developed agriculture,

were of a poor order. The Aztecs' dependence on rain is the
"reason why" for the ceaseless preoccupation with the ap-
peasement of the gods and with conquests, the wars for more
tribute and for more sacrificial victims in order to cajole the
rain god into proffering the withheld gifts of rain. As the
good will of the rain god could only be sustained by a diet
of human hearts, and as these could only be provided by
taking prisoners in battle, a long peace was a disaster. Only
in perpetual war was there safety.

It was a nightmare.

14. Tax Contributions to the State

Even in such a moneyless society as the Aztec, everything, unfortunately, had to be paid for; taxes and death to the common Aztec *macehualli* were as inevitable as conception. Babylon invented money, this symbol that simplified life all over the world. But because of geographic isolation, no civilization in prehistoric America knew money, if one excepts the use of cacao money. "The Cacao is a fruit little lesse than almonds," José de Acosta tells us. "They use it in steede of money for with five cacaos they buy one thing, with thirtie another and with a hundred another, without any contradiction . . . from it theye make a drincke which they call Chocolate."

Taxes, whatever the reality of cacao money, were paid in service and seem to have been assessed through the clan. "The tribal council divided the land among the clans and the leaders of each in turn apportioned its share among the heads of families justly and equitably." [81] Sections were also reserved for the maintenance of the chief of the temple staff, for war supplies, and for the payment of tribute. Other portions of this land controlled directly by the clan were worked communally and the yield—whether corn, beans, or agave fibers—was paid as tribute-tax to the central tribal council for the maintenance of religion, war, the "king" and his various non-taxpaying staff, (priests, army, craftsmen, concubines, keepers of the royal aviary), and for the engineering works in and beyond Mexico-Tenochtitlán and all the other paraphernalia of state with which we today are so fully familiar.

In addition to the foodstuffs which were sent to the central granaries and noted down in the account books by the Tribute Recorder of the Chief Speaker, the clan group was also called upon for levies of manpower to build public buildings. Under direction from architect-builders, who were tax-exempt, dikes, aqueducts, roads were built. The "king" of the Aztecs also had lands which were cultivated by clans in rotation, and the yield of this also went into the official deposits.

"Tell me what you eat, and I will tell you what you are," wrote Anthelme Brillat-Savarin in his *Physiologie du Goût,* written in Connecticut while he waited for the French Revolution to burn itself out. This aphorism could apply to all Neolithic theocracies, especially the Aztec. Frequent comparisons have been made between the temple-cities in America and those in Sumer. In primitive societies all were farmers, for "in a hypothetical pure Neolithic economy there would be no full-time specialist." [16] When farming improved, a surplus was produced and granaries were attached to the temples, in Sumer as in America. As man became completely dependent on agriculture and since sun and rain were derived from the gods, who "owned" the soil they tilled, the first fruit "tithes," in Christian parlance, were given to the temple to support the galaxy of priests who acted as the intermediaries for the gods. These surpluses were used to aggrandize the temple, secure the interest of the priestly class, and provide exchange for the import of raw materials they lacked. The administration of all this produced the temple-city, and so there came into being the specialists: craftsmen, administrators, clerks (*tlacuilo* writers in Mexico), who put down receipts and expenditures. These early temple accounts are among the oldest cuneiform writing in Sumer (3500 B.C.), and their Aztec counterparts constituted, until they were destroyed, some of the oldest Aztec records.

It is obvious that the directing class themselves did not personally consume all that poured into Mexico-Tenochtitlán. The surplus was used to compensate the specialists. It was also stored for general use during crop failures. Since accounts had to be kept, some archaeologists believe this was one of the factors which brought about the invention of writing.*

That the Incas, who also had a tribute state, should have developed only the *quipu* and not writing, remains one of the earth's mysteries.

* V. Gordon Childe writes that the "standardization of conventional graphic system" stimulated the invention of writing. "The art of reading and writing [he is writing about the lands of Mesopotamia] became an accomplishment with considerable prestige. The initiates were exempted from all manual tasks." Further, they were trusted with the task of thinking for the society. This was duplicated in Aztec society.

15.   The Loom—A Woman's Art

WEAVING was one of the functions that belonged wholly to woman.

She gathered the fiber, prepared it, spun, dyed, and then loomed it; no male interfered. It is a fact sometimes overlooked that, in this strange world where everyone was a craftsman in one form or another, the anonymous and communal weaving artisans were all women. Theirs was also an ephemeral art. None of the millions of pieces loomed has survived and all we know of Aztec design is that which has come down to us in the Book of Tributes or else what was painted on pottery and on murals.

The Aztec backstrap loom was simple. The type is known, with little variation, throughout all the Americas. Two wooden rods are fastened, one to each end of the warp, to stretch the cloth to desired length; the lower one is attached to the back of the weaver (hence the name "backstrap"), while the upper is tied to a post or tree. Three feet wide, the warp was loomed by means of a shuttle woven between the strands of the stretched yarn: that simple. And yet from these looms came, if one can trust the enthusiasm of the conquistadors, some of the finest weavings they had ever seen. "Eight damsels, they were," wrote Bernal Díaz, "all eight of them clothed in the rich garments of the country, beautifully ornamented. . . ."

The Aztecs when they were wanderers used the fiber of the maguey (*metl*), a spined succulent which, after corn, was one of Mexico's most beneficent plants. It provided them with intoxicating drink (*octli*), rope fiber, which, under the name "henequen," is a well-known commercial product, and numerous other products too many and too varied to be noted here. This agave was a primary source of fiber. The pad (technically it is not a leaf) of this succulent is veined with strong fibers, which, when dried, combed, and spun, can be made sufficiently delicate to spin; from this fiber of the

81

24. *Weaving was the woman's art. At the left, she uses the typical backstrap loom; to the right, carded cotton is put into thread on a spindle whorl which rests in a ceramic bowl.*

maguey, a very coarse linenlike thread, the Aztec women made their first weavings. Later, when they rose in social scale and could barter, they obtained cotton from the warmer valleys. Cotton soon passed from a luxury to a necessity, and one of the principal errands of their traders, who went to the south hotlands for goods or tribute, was to obtain the indispensable cotton. Women bartered for cotton in the market, or, when it arrived as tribute, it was distributed equally to the clans and each woman weaver obtained her share.

Cotton fibers were spun on the traditional spindle, a slender wooden stick ten to twelve inches in length, balanced at the lower end by a pottery whorl. This is "traditional" in that wherever there has been spinning and weaving the ancient technique of fiber preparation has been the same. It would be a well-versed archaeologist who could differentiate between the spindle rings of Palestine (3000 B.C.); Troy (2500 B.C.); Peru (2000 B.C.); Maya (200 B.C.), or Aztec (A.D. 1300). Curiously enough, all that is left of the greatest art of Mexico and Yucatán is the ceramic spindle whorl. All else—weavings, loom, even the sticks—has succumbed to time. The method of spinning the fiber, with the "business end" left in a small ceramic bowl, has been pictured by the Aztecs themselves.

The fibers after spinning were dyed, with urine as mordant to fix the color. Dyes were mostly vegetable: *achiotl* (the *Bixa* genus) yielded red—this, under the name of *anatto*, was later used in our own economy to dye oleomargarine; anil, a shrub, gave a dark blue; cochineal, a scale insect parasite, was gathered, as its Latin name, *coccus cacti,* implies, on the cactus by Indians, who obtained from it a carmine color; and there were others. The dark seed of the genipa, found on a tree in the hotlands, yielded a black color; a lavender color came, like the "royal purple of Tyre," from a mollusk found along the Pacific coast.

Color was more than color. It was symbolism, and, to the Aztec, very real. If red was used as blood, it became the actual equivalent of blood; it *was* blood. Black represented war because black obsidian glass was the cutting edge of battle swords (*maquahuitl*); it was also the symbol of religion: the priests dressed exclusively in it. Yellow was food because it was the color of corn; blue meant sacrifice; and green was royal, because it was the color of the quetzal plumes used only by chieftains. The French symbolists led by Mallarmé at the end of the nineteenth century used color in the same way in their poetry. And when they assailed all Paris with the allegories and esotericism of these ancient theurgies, what they believed to be so new was in reality as old as the world itself.

Design had no horizons—everything was allowed, everything permitted. Protected by the goddess Xochiquetzal, the weaver expressed anything that she felt. Of nature and realism, there were the things of the earth—sun, fish, snails, cactus, bird feathers, tiger skins, even falling snow were used as motifs; there were geometric designs, highly stylized animals, transformation of representational art into allover patterns. All this is suggested in the designs taken from the Book of Tributes and redrawn from the actual weavings delivered to Mexico-Tenochtitlán.

For themselves women wove the skirts ankle length, elaborately bordered, and for the top part of the costume the well-known *huipilli*. Their art sense ran riot. The striking effect of the women's dress was not exaggerated by the conquistador. Consider this description by a padre during the festivals of the month when the women, especially the beautifully dressed concubines, danced with the soldiers: ". . . and all were well clothed, beautifully adorned, all had wonderfully wrought skirts and pretty *huipilli*. The skirts were decorated with designs representing hearts, others a fish motif, others with spirals or leaves, some were of a simple weave; they all had frames, hems, and fringes. . . . As to the blouses, some had loose dark adornments, others motifs representing smoke or black stripes and some with houses or fishes. . . ." [69]

For the men, women wove two principal garments: the breech-clout (*maxtli*), a single piece with highly decorated ends which went about the waist, and a long cloak (*tilmantli*), which knotted at the shoulder, since they had neither brooches, pins, nor buttons. A portrait of Nezahualpilli, "king" of Texcoco, an ally of Tenochtitlán, shows such a costume elaborated for so exalted a person.

War kept the women further occupied. They wove a coarse cloth of cotton for the war dress (*xicolli*), and also, as a protection against arrows, a quilted cotton jacket not unlike that which the Chinese use against the cold. These jackets the Spaniards thought superior to their own steel armor.

The priests wore ankle-length black ponchos and got them from the looms of young virgins assigned to the temples. As befitting the necromancy of their beliefs, they were bordered with skulls and crossbones.

16. Pottery and Pottery Makers

POTTERY, like weaving and housebuilding, was part of the Aztec cultural equipment. All made pottery in one form or another even if all did not make *fine* pottery. This self-sufficiency is what prompted Aldous Huxley in his Mexican travels to cite "the primitive's human wholeness." [43] Pottery making confirms the point that "a primitive is forced to be whole—a complete man, trained in all the skills of the community . . . if he is not whole, he perishes." All of the tribes were pottery makers, those of Cholula being especially famed for their red and black ware. It was mostly a craft industry done at home with the leisure time allowed from agriculture. A number of pottery makers who rose in public esteem as artisans left agriculture entirely and organized the guild of pottery makers. Utilitarian pottery, coarse-grained and designed for heavy duty, was used for cooking. Three-legged pots, the large *cumal* which was a flat disk-shaped griddle for baking tortillas, bowls with roughened surface to act as graters for braying chili peppers—these, with pottery goblets for pulque, were part of every household. The finer pieces of delicate pottery almost as thin as good china, the beautifully decorated kind the archaeologists find in graves, were for the dead.

There was more to pottery than mere pots and drinking bowls. Spindle whorls, which weighted the spinning distaff like a flywheel, and spinning sticks too, were made of clay. Ceramic dolls were made with jointed arms. Toys were made with wheels, although the idea of putting the wheel to any other use never occurred to them. The little clay gods, gods of fertility and corn, were mass-produced in clay forms; the cult figurine was dropped by the farmer into his cornfield to conjure the good will of the local genii for a better corn crop. Each household had its charcoal brazier to snuff out the chill, and temples had large ceramic braziers the height of a man, coalescing beauty and utility, a ritualistic

25. *Aztec ceramics. These are the types that were made for use and export at the height of Aztec power. The long-handled ceramic was used by priests in the burning of* copal *to remove disease of newness. The other vessels were for eating and drinking.*

usefulness with architectural ornament; there were clay stamps and seals used for stamping cloth and *amatl* paper, a step in the evolution of printing. After ideographic writing, the next inevitable step (as the Chinese saw it) was to reduce the ideograph to a symbol and "print"— impress the seal on paper. Thus with these pottery stamps and *amatl* paper they were very close to true printing.

Pottery, apart from its beauty of form, provides an important record to the archaeologist. Potsherds may be dismal to read about and equally dismal to work over but they represent a type of history. A preliterate people give more precise information in their pottery than in their legends and architecture. Much can be determined from the stylistic changes effected in pottery. A new god cult arrives, a new epoch is ushered in, a new age—it is first reflected in pottery. A conqueror comes, and the temples remain standing, but the common people echo the change—we have seen the same thing in our late wars—reflecting the conqueror in style of clothes, manners, habits; pottery provides the sequence of advance and decline. By using potsherds to establish spatial relationships, the archaeologist uses some of the techniques of geology: a stratigraphical cut at the kitchen midden of an archaeological site reveals the debris of the process of living. Pottery products are mixed with all the other artifacts and are imperishable. In painting, design, materials, techniques, they reveal age and establish a relative chronology.

Pottery was functional in this society of craftsmen. It brought psychological fulfillment—handicrafts are one of the therapeutic techniques of the psychiatrist. It has social utility—an economy based upon handicraft culture is not so liable to fluctuations as one based on mass-produced products. The Aztecs, who knew nothing of such reasoning, thought only of using the surplus pottery production as an exchange medium at the weekly market.

26. *Various other pottery forms used in Aztec households. These were all utilitarian and were not placed in graves or tombs.*

17. *Tiaquiz:* The Market

THE MARKET was like Napoleon's measure of Switzerland; if such a thing did not exist it would have to be invented—an uninvolved ground in which warring nations trade. The idea that trade is sacrosanct is as old as society itself; the market did not have to be invented; it came into being wherever man lived and traded, sold and bartered. Yet even so the Mexican market was astonishing.

"When we arrived at the great market place," remembered the chronicler,[25] ". . . we were astounded at the number of people and the quantity of merchandise . . . and at the good order and control that was maintained. . . ." "Yes," agreed Hernán Cortés after visiting the same market, "there are daily more than sixty thousand people bartering and selling . . . the square is twice as big as Salamanca . . . every kind of merchandise . . . is for sale. . . . There is a street of game [partridges, turkeys, quail, pigeons, parrots, owls, kestrels]. . . . There is a street of herb sellers . . . roots and . . . medicinal herbs . . . and houses of the apothecaries in which they sell the medicines from these herbs. . . . There are barber shops where you may have your hair washed and cut." And, as if they vied with each other, Bernal Díaz recalled "other wares," i.e., "Indian slaves [*tlacotli*] both men and women [brought in] as the Portuguese bring negroes from Guinea . . . tied to long poles. . . ." Next there were "traders who sold great pieces of . . . cotton, and articles of twisted thread. . . ." Much in evidence was the coarse cloth spun from the fibers of the maguey and used by those who carried cargo on their backs, and the sandals made of the same fiber. Cortés wrote of the various animal skins for sale and the pottery "of very good quality"; and his companion asked that they not forget the "paper" offered for sale, ". . . which in this country is called *amatl*, and reeds scented with *liquidambar* . . . and tobacco . . . much cochineal . . . I am forgetting those who

27. *Activity at the* tiaquiz *(market) covered all the phases of Aztec life, interest, and consumption. Women are seen bargaining for food, men for luxuries.*

sell salt and those who make the stone knives. . . ." There were "dealers in gold, silver [this would have been impossible in Peru where the Lord-Inca 'owned' all metals], and precious stones, feathers, mantles. . . ." And along with all this commercial activity, there was order. "A very fine building," Cortés assured his liege, Charles V, "stands in the great square and serves as a kind of audience where ten or twelve persons are always seated, as judges, who deliberate on all cases arising in the market and pass instant sentences on wrongdoers."

Such was the market (*tiaquiz*), of which there were five on the island. Every city on the mainland had its own *tiaquiz*, and the festive days were so arranged that the people could attend the various ones within the circuit of the valley of Anáhuac.

While the Mexican market was large, perhaps the greatest, it was not unique: the market at Cholula was a mecca because of its great temple to Quetzalcoatl, which drew people from all over Mexico. Even those who were traditional enemies held their enmities in abeyance while they carried on trade. Trade was sacred. The Spaniards who on their march to Mexico entered Tlascala, a tribal state in perpetual war with the Aztecs, found a city which Cortés thought "larger than Granada . . . with a market in which more than thirty thousand people daily are occupied in buying and selling . . . nothing is lacking. There are gold, silver and precious stones and jewellers' 'shops' . . . there is earthenware . . . as fine as any in Spain . . . there are booths for washing your hair and barbers to shave you . . . there are also public baths . . . and good order for . . . they behave like a people of sense and reason . . . the foremost city of Africa cannot rival them."

If marching meant markets, men marched. It is incredible, until one sifts the evidence, the distances men walked from the earliest times to market surplus and buy up their lack. Long before 2500 B.C., man in many parts of the world was going to the markets. "The extreme parts of the inhabitable world," wrote the Greek historian Herodotus, who visited many of them himself, "possess the most excellent products." All of the early routes were luxury routes and the markets were luxury markets. Persia's roads were crowded "with men on the king's business"; people were drawn to trade in the remote Indus valley so early that when Alexander the Great ventured into it expecting something else "he found well-made roads built of clay-brick" and all manner of "trees bearing yellow fruits lining the way." Whether it was early China trade or the Danube traffic or the Fertile Crescent which drew man, all were bent on ridding themselves of surplus and gaining luxuries. Trade was the loadstone that drew man to its world markets.

The Aztec market, which included tribute in its wares, differed little in the beginning from the usual "American" system of war tribute. But the Aztecs systematized it, and every six months 371 vassal cities yielded tribute of products so varied and vast that elaborate account books were needed to keep track of it. The market was further fed by the activities of its wandering merchants. Bernal Díaz himself said: "But why do I waste so many words in recounting what they sell in that great market?—for I shall never finish if I tell it all in detail."

18. The Festival Days

THE FESTIVAL was almost continuous in ancient Mexico. It is not easy to separate festive and ceremonial, sacred and secular, since everything was bound up together. It is not difficult, however, to find a parallel in times not far distant when hangings and garrotings were always an occasion for holidays, and to realize how, in affairs of this kind, festival and sacred ritual were interlocked.

Like all other advanced tribes, the Aztecs had a calendar, divided into eighteen 20-day months; every one of these eighteen months had ceremonies and festivals. Months had descriptive names. The first month was Atlcoulaco ("want of water") and there were ceremonies, parades, and sacrifice. The second month was Tlacaxipeualiztli ("boning of the men"), when for sixteen days there were ceremonies and parades with priests dancing in the flayed skins of sacrificial victims. This skin, naturally, had magic powers—it gave to the priest who danced in it the power of the undead (i.e., the sacrificial victim whose skin it was); nor was this skin merely a symbol, something that prefigures, as a symbol is to us—it was consubstantiality. We can grasp some of the meaning of this, perhaps, in the story told by Anatole France of an eighteenth-century burgher of Séez who was robbed of some doubloons by his servant. Knowing his rights, he exacted the skin of the thief after she had been tried and executed, and made pantaloons from it, and whenever the thought of his loss overcame him, he would smack his thigh and cry, "The hussy. The hussy."

The third month, Tozoztontli, began with "fasting," and if this did not touch the heart of the rain god, Tlaloc, another festival, the flayed-skin dance to Xipé was performed by the priests. The fourth month brought the people into the city from the fields to celebrate the worship of the new corn; altars in their houses were festooned with cornstalks. This was a bloodless time and young girls gave virginal blessings to the seed corn. By the fifth month (May 3–22) rain was full upon them; there were god-impersonation ceremonies, and they sacri-

28. *The flywheel, a game-ceremony in which men, dressed as birds, hung from ropes and rotated, giving the effect of flight. This is still performed in some parts of Mexico.*

ficed children to the rain god to thank him (they had
sacrificed children in the third month to bring on the rain).
It is of course pure calumny to say that anthropophagy was
involved in this, although Bernal Díaz wrote: "I have
heard it said that they were wont to cook for Moctezuma
the flesh of young boys." If that occurred at all, it was a ceremonial cannibalism.

The seventh month (June 12–July 1) was marked with the
mimic dances of the salt workers, who leeched salt from
the lakes of Anáhuac. The eighth month (July 2–21) was a
joyous one—the adoration of the eating of the corn, an
eight-day feast which could not get under way until the
priests had dispatched a slave girl, beautifully attired to impersonate the Goddess of Young Corn. The ninth month,
Tlaxochimaco ("birth of flowers"), brought feasts which
lasted some days and was unusual in that the two sexes
danced together, "even touching the women," as an old Aztec
explained. It was the rising class of merchant prince
(*pochteca*) that gave these feasts, appropriately, for at the
end it was to their god, Yacatecuhtli, protector of merchants.

The tenth month (August 11–30) was ostensibly to cele-

29. *Jugglers and musicians enlivened the festive days. Jesters
and "merry-andrews" were part of the equipment of a high-
placed Aztec.*

30. *The dance of Xocotlhuetzi. This took place in the month of that name, which celebrated the "fall of fruits." Men danced about a tree ornamented with paper flags. From the* Codex Mendoza.

brate the "fall of the fruits." The people poured in in a festive mood, much as they once did in Europe to see someone
drawn and quartered or, even better, beheaded. One has only
to see Jacques Callot's mischievous drawings of the people
of Paris rollicking during an execution to see the intermingling of holiday and bloodletting. In the Aztec world the rites
to the fire god, Huehueteotl, were also certain to attract
holiday crowds. Prisoners of war danced together with their
captors and then, according to Dr. Vaillant, ascended to the
top of a platform where *yauhtli* powder, an analgesic, was
blown on their faces to anesthetize them somewhat during
the next minutes. The half-awake prisoners were whirled
about a dazzling fire and then dumped into the coals, fished
out while still alive to have their still palpitating hearts cut
out to be offered to the gods. There followed, after food
and libations of intoxicating *octli,* a competitive climbing
of a pole about fifty feet high to retrieve various paper in-
signia on top of it.

The eleventh month, from the end of August until September 19, was Ochpaniztli ("month of brooms"), with, of course,
the usual sacrifices. It was also a military month with a re-
view of all the clans parading with new arms, their own in-
signia on their shields; there was a procession of the knights
of the Eagle and the knights of the Jaguar (who wore the
animal skins as battle dress), a phalanx of warriors with
special privileges; the festival ended in a gladiatorial con-
test.

The twelfth month, Teotleco, marked the return of the
gods to earth (*teo,* "god," *tleco,* "return") and good fun for
young and old, for ceremonial drunkenness was the rule of
the day.

The thirteenth (October 10–29) had to do with Tlaloc,
the demanding god. The fourteenth involved a general penance for four days; men were expected to abstain, with ceremony or without it, from their wives. Panquetzaliztli ("feast
of the flags"), which was celebrated as the fifteenth month,
honored the war god first with mock battles; then, says
Sahagún, "the women sang and danced . . . intermingling
with the men. . . ." They poured jugs of water over their
heads—much as was done in the carnivals in Lima—took
off their wet clothes, dyed their arms and legs blue, and
dressed in *amatl* paper. The people marked for sacrifice also
dressed in paper. It was raining again by the sixteenth month
(December 9–28), and the month's name, Atemoztli, meant
"fall of waters." The people prepared themselves by fasting

five days previous to this feast. They spent the entire night cutting *amatl* paper "in diverse shapes, stuck them on poles, put them up in their homes and invited the symbol of the image they had cut to come together." They made vows, says Sahagún, "and at the same time took to their drums, their jingles and their tortoise-shell to play on." The seventeenth month brought the cold—it was the end of December. Now they tried to touch the rain god's heart, to persuade him to give them the withheld gift of rain. First the women wept, then the men; the men pelted their women with straw-filled bags to hurry on the tears. The eighteenth, the last month of the year, was to Izcalli. It was a time of mass sacrifice. The women who were to be immolated were dressed in *amatl* paper clothing, and after that they repaired to Cuauhtitlán, where prisoners of war were lashed to scaffolds, after the manner of the Pawnees of the western plains, and killed with arrows.

In all, the eighteen 20-day Aztec months accounted for 360 days. The imagination could not encompass more. It was satiated. There followed the *nemontemi,* the "five empty days" (February 7–11). One did nothing . . . no fire, no music no love . . . one sat huddled waiting, waiting. . . .

To picture the life of the Aztec as one long joyous idyl cadenced by the beat of the drum to the frenzied dance of priests would, as one sees in this chapter, be wide of the mark. The Aztecs were terrorized as much by life as by the elements. The phenomenon of a snowstorm—understandably at 7,400 feet altitude—caused them to search their souls for portents; an involuntary loss of blood was disastrous; any contact with woman's catamenial flux would set off a concatenation of disasters.

Tenochtitlán may have been a paradise, but it was troubled one.

19. Music

Aztec music—indeed all of American music—was tied up with dancing; any "pure" music has disappeared. What remains suggests that Aztec music was strong in rhythm but lacking in tone. This, at least, is what one infers from the instruments: the large upright drum, skin stretched over wood frame (*huehuetl*), was beaten with the bare hands and some control was exercised on the beat and quality of the tone; a smaller counterpart was hung around the neck and beaten with both hands, but contact with the body spoiled the resonance; the two-note wooden drum (*teponzatli*) was beaten with rubber-tipped beaters, sonorous but monotonous. The conch shell—all peoples who have had contact with the sea have had the conch, including the Inca and its use seems to have been world-wide—gave out an impressively deep blast: a chorus of them were used early in the morning with the rising of Venus to arouse the people out of sleep. Since they had no string instruments nor such instruments as the marimba—these were cultural borrowings from Negro slaves—their forte was the percussion instrument in various forms. They also had flutes shaped like Panpipes, in clay or of reed, and whistles, and in addition to the rattles, seed-filled gourds, and the seed or shell attachments on the ankles that kept the beat. These are still used by the present-day Yaqui people. There were also notched bones, usually human femurs, which, rasped with a stick, suggest modern *musica Cubana*. The thing to note was that the music was rhythmic, not melodic; its outward effect was cadence to the dancer, its inward effect, hypnotic.

Dance was as inseparable from music as was singing or rhythmic stress. There were mass dances of various forms and there were certainly group dances. But, warriors or priests, merchants or chiefs—under whatever guise—the dance had but one function: to obtain aid from the unseen powers upon which Aztec prosperity depended. Drunkenness

31. *Music and musical instruments. Trumpet, drum, and gourd rattles produced the principal effects. The Aztec at the left blows a conch horn. The next man beats a* huehuetl, *an upright drum of stretched skin. Another beats a two-noted wooden* teponzatli *(the beaters were of rubber). The dancing figure shakes the gourd rattles.*

itself was ritual and sacred. The dance with music was to seduce the gods; the fundamental, the *raison d'étre*, of the dance, to the dancers as well as the watchers, was "mystic communion," the fusion which made them one with the god they hoped would hear their call. Drumming was of supreme importance: it soothed the soul and made the gods amenable. Drumming also exerted a real mystical influence; it acted upon the disposition of the unseen as it acted upon the spectator, so that from the "mystic point of view the drum was an indispensable part of the magico-propitiatory apparatus." [52]

Drum and song were acclaimed together. With the beat of the bass drum and the two-noted wooden drums giving the added dignity of background, the singer (*cuicani*) gave out this to the national Aztec god:

> *I am Hummingbird Wizard, the warrior, no one is equal to myself.*

*Not in vain have I donned my robe of yellow feathers;
for me the sun has arisen.*

Song, music, rhythm, in addition to breaking the dull
monotony of their lives, were used, as they always have
been, for memory. There was little doubt of the effect sought
after by the Aztec impresario. The various episodes of
the dance, the same movements repeated without number,
the volumes of sound, the ornaments and masks, all had one
aim, one religious aim—emotional paroxysms in which all
present were robbed of their self-possession and thus believed
that their wish to secure the favor of the gods had been attained.

20. Games

GAMES have always been immense fun. But to the Aztecs the "game" was not enough in itself. As with the present-day Russians, it was for them serious business, magical and ritualistic; it had no point of rest. They were more earnest in what was supposed to be unserious than in serious matters. This finds a counterpart in the pages of Anatole France's *La Rôtisserie de la reine Pédauque*, where, in a highly amusing card-playing scene, the author reflects that "men are more punctilious at play then in serious matters and they bring more honesty to bear on tric-trac where it is passable hindrance and leave it out in battles or in treaties of peace where it would be troublesome."

The passions which man displays in games were best seen in a game played from Honduras to Arizona and known as *tlachtli*. It began as a sport; it ended up as ritual. No one can say precisely where or when it began, except that the Olmecs who lived in the hotlands of the Gulf Coast, where rubber* grew, had the game as early as 500 B.C.—a ball court was found in their temple complex at La Venta—and their name was derived from the word for rubber, *olli* (*Ol-mec*: "rubber people").

Tlachtli was then already formalized. Yet the expressive pre-Aztec clay figures of tribesmen playing a variant of the game show it was as popular and ritualistic as baseball—if one must have an analogy. It was played in a court shaped like an *I*; walls of tiered seats were on either side. In the middle of this was the "basket," a stone or wooden ring set, not horizontally as in basketball, but vertically; the object was to put the rubber ball through the ring. The ball was hard,

---

* Charles Marie de La Condamine (1701–74) was the first to experiment with rubber. He found it in use as a sort of syringe by Indians in the Amazon. Rubber from Vera Cruz was first mentioned by Oviedo, the Spanish historiographer, in 1500.

not inflated. The players were allowed to strike it only with legs or hips or elbows; they were padded like a goalie in ice hockey. Although many played it, *tlachtli* was essentially a religious game performed before the rulers of tribes. In Mexico-Tenochtitlán, the ball court stood in the sacred enclosure in front of the racks of skulls of those who had been sacrificed at the main temple and was bounded on one side by the temple dedicated to the knights of the Eagle.

The Friar Bernardino de Sahagún wrote of the game: "the balls were about the size of bowling balls [i.e., six inches in diameter] and were solid, made of a gum called *ulli* . . . which is very light and bounces like an inflated ball." In playing, both players and spectators placed enormous bets, "gold, turquoise, slaves, rich mantles, even cornfields and houses [which reminds one that Cardinal Mazarin lost an entire chateau in a single play of bezique] . . . at other times the lord played ball for his pastime . . . he also brought with him good ball players who played before him, and other principal men played on the opposite team, and they won gold and *chalchiguites* and beads of gold, and tur-

32. Tlachtli *was the first basketball game. Popular as well as ritualistic, it was played in a rectangular court with stone "baskets" placed vertically. The ball was of hard rubber. The game was known and played from Honduras to Arizona.*

quoise and slaves and rich mantles and maxtles and cornfields and houses, etc. [feathers, cacao, cloaks of feather]
. . . the ball court . . . consisted of two walls, twenty or thirty
feet apart, that were up to forty or fifty feet in length; the
walls . . . were whitewashed and about eight and a half
feet high, and in the middle of the court was a line which
was used in the game . . . in the middle of the walls, in
the center of the court, were two stones, like millstones
hollowed out, opposite each other, and each one had a hole
wide enough to contain the ball. . . . And the one who put
the ball in it won the game. They did not play with their
hands, but instead struck the ball with their buttocks; for
playing they wore gloves on their hands and a belt of leather
on their buttocks, with which to strike the ball."

In other games also the Aztecs were certainly as "punctil-

33. Patolli, *a game utilizing a board shaped like a cross, was
played something like parchesi. Although a game of chance
and used for gambling,* patolli *was semisacred and was watched
over by Macuilxochitl, the Five-flower Goddess.*

ious in play as in serious matters." *Patolli*, something like backgammon or parchesi, was a less sanguine sport and was played on a marked board or paper, with beans for counters. The object was to travel about the board and return "home" to win. It is doubtless the same game that Cortés used to play with Moctezuma when he was the Spaniards' captive in his own palace. Bernal Díaz called it *totoloque*. It was a gambling game, as he said, played "with some very smooth pellets made of gold. . . . They toss these pellets some distance as well as some little slabs which were also made of gold. . . . In five strokes or tries they gained or lost certain pieces of gold or rich jewels that they staked." *

There were other games, mostly played by children, that have their counterparts in our own life. But all this was the playtime of the little man before ritual and the gloomy pessimism of Aztec life turned his naturally gay exuberance into something lugubrious.

* There were only two players but each had his own official scorekeeper. Cortés had Pedro de Alvarado (called "the Sun" by the Aztec because of his white-blond hair), and Moctezuma observed that Alvarado always marked more points than Cortés gained and "courteously and laughingly he said he was being done ill because Cortés was making so much *yxoxol* in the game," i.e., he was cheating.

21. The Expediency of Justice

"CODES OF LAW," said Rabelais when he stopped panta-gruelizing long enough to be very serious, "are founded upon necessity and not upon justice." And the Aztecs would have agreed. They were not versed in the dialects of "as if"; their justice was exacting, swift, and final. What was crime? Stealing, adultery, blasphemy, killing, and drunkenness (unless it was ritual). All these were capital crimes. It

34. *Aztec justice as shown in the* Codex Florentino *and drawn by an Aztec artist. Three chieftains condemn a criminal for an outrageous crime and witness his execution by garroting.*

is difficult to understand that a nation given to such overwhelming sacrificial slaughter would be so aghast at death. But there was a fundamental difference: war and ceremonial sacrifice, murder and rape during battle did not involve the clan or tribe. This does not differ in practice from our own moral phenomena—"There is no such thing as moral phenomena, only a moral interpretation of phenomena"; we reward the killer during war and consider murder beyond the pale during peace.

Aztec society, as do all societies, existed (in theory and mostly in practice) for the benefit of its component parts. The Aztec ideas of justice were ancient. Stealing to them was an aberration, for which restitution in kind was the usual penance. For things that could not be restored, there was death or else expulsion from the clan (the same thing) or into slavery. Adultery brought death, although this varied much with the circumstances of the people involved. Punishment to tribesmen who misused the "king's way," the Aztec road, was severe; robbery of merchants carrying on "sacred business" was death by stoning—commerce and the royal way were sacrosanct. The penalty for murder naturally was death.

The most heinous were religious crimes. The robbing of temples, an offense that might provoke the disfavor of the gods, or doubting the efficacy of prayers, in short to blaspheme (to blame) anything that might bring disaster on the whole tribe—this brought immediate death. It was no different in the Christian world; an auto-da-fé reported from Seville in the *Fugger News-Letters* in 1579: "sentence the *third;* Juan de Color, slave, 35, reviled the name of Our Dear Lady and other saints—disputed her miracles . . . burning at the stake."

Witchcraft was the deadliest of crimes. Obsession with it is interwoven in the deepest fibers of the primitive mind, especially if it was directed toward someone of one's own clan. It was the worst crime that one could commit, and to cause death by witchcraft was considered worse than murder—it was anthropophagy, i.e., the eating of kin's flesh. The sentence of death was carried out only after protracted torture. To remain impartial, however, we must recall the prevalence of witches in our own world. There was the notorious witch Walpurga Hausmann, who, as reported in one of the *Fugger News-Letters,* confessed in 1587 to killing forty-three children over a period of thirty years. The bishop of Augsburg gave the verdict: "despatch from life by burning. . . ." And the verdict on another tried for misdeeds of witchcraft was changed to "as the result of her fervent petitioning her sentence has been lightened . . . first she will be strangled and only then burned."

The administration of justice was designed so that people would live in harmony among themselves. (It was not designed for their neighbors, for all other men were enemies.)

They lived by a code far more strict than the one we impose on ourselves. In the eternal theater of carnage and death that was Aztec, one had to conform.

22. Medicinal Plants

MEDICINAL PLANTS in the Aztec world were of a wide and interesting order. Few protohistoric peoples have left so extensive a description of plants, economic, aesthetic, and curative. The Aztecs, like all other "Mexicans" before them, were metaphysicians far more spontaneous than we ourselves. They wore amulets to protect against disease— an arm stricture, a nose ornament, a lucky shell or stone, a talisman to avert a baleful influence. Diseases, numbered among the disasters, were caused by unseen powers; defense was made by appealing to the same medium. Although not completely unaware of the pathological, their medicine was bound up with magic and religion. Yet since life is a lying dream and physics often saves one from metaphysics, the Aztecs, who were good herbalists, applied what they knew to ease the disease.

The cure doctor (*ticitl*) appeared in cases of serious illness; he brought with him all the appurtenances of the shaman (in the theatrical world, "props")—shells, eagle wings, a hank of hair, tobacco to purify by smoke. He began as a masseur by rubbing on the body to find and extract the "fairy dart"—a stone, a rock, a small arrow—which had entered the body and "caused" the illness. One of the names of the cure doctor comes from this: *tetla-acuicilique*, "he-who-recovers-the-stone." Illness was not natural; it had a mystical cause. It was carried down from the mountain on winds (we believed the tertiary fevers came from the bad air; hence "malaria"); or Tlaloc, the rain god, for a lack of proper obeisance, sent leprosy, ulcers, even foot trouble (a disaster to people who were their own draft animals); or if man and woman in love breached the tabu of incest, they could die of *tlazol-miquiztli*, "love death." The best cure for such cravings was to invoke the name of the genie of desire, one Tlazol-teteo, and take a hot steam bath (not much different from the method described in the limerick "by thinking of Jesus/ and

35. *The cure doctor* (ticitl) *at work. An old woman, as shown in the* Codex Florentino, *applies leaves to the back of a young mother.*

and veneral diseases/ and the risk of begetting a child").

If the cause of the disease, after the magical object had been removed, was not easily diagnosed, the witch doctor gave the patient an infusion of the bark of *oloiuhqui*. Since this is of the *Datura* family and possesses narcotic properties, the patient dreamed and talked and supposedly revealed the cause of his illness. (The same principle underlies narcosynthesis treatment in modern medicine.) Once the hocus-pocus was over, the cure doctor used remedies, some sensible, others ineffectual, and still others (as in our own world) ridiculous and even harmful. Whatever it was, the Indian patient accepted it without protest, afraid to modify it by complaining and so spoiling its miraculous powers.

What were the diseases they had to cure? About the same as afflicted most of the indigenous Americans before white man's arrival: colds, grippe, and all the other respiratory diseases; malaria; swarms of intestinal infections and infestations; leprosy; skin diseases; and—most probably—syphilis.

The Aztec herbalists worked out a classification of plants, particularly of those having therapeutic value. Much of this information, fortunately, was gathered before time and the effect of conquest brought the society to an end. There are a few such herbals extant, *The de la Cruz-Badiano Aztec Herbal,* for instance, written in 1552.

The herbalist had a full command of curatives, as was known to José de Acosta, the learned Jesuit who traveled in Mexico in 1565: "I say onely that in the time of . . . the Mexican Kings, there were many great personages expert in curing of diseases with simples . . . having the knowledge of the many vertues and properties of hearbes, roots, woodes and plants. . . . There are a thousand of these simples fit to purge, as the rootes of *Guanucchoacan,* the *Pignons of Punua,* the conserve of *Guanucquo,* the oyle of Fig-trees. . . ."

They were, like all such Homeric simples, formed of equal portions of cure, hope, and magic. For boils take the leaves of the *tlatl-anquaye* root, apply morning and noon, wash after the application with urine. Loss of hair could be prevented by a lotion of dog's or deer's urine with the plant called *xiuh-amolli.* If the head was broken in battle, "The break should be smeared with plants growing in summer dew, with green-stone pearls, crystal and the *tlaca-huatzin,* and with wormy earth, ground up in the blood from a bruised vein and the white of an egg; if blood cannot be had burned frogs will take the place." [35] The cures suggest the

36. *Mexican medicinal plants. From an Aztec herbal. On the left is* Peyotl; *on the right* elo-xochitl.

diseases that afflicted the Aztec: he ate too much corn, too little meat, not enough greenstuffs; the tropics brought their toll of intestinal diseases; birth was not always as easy as it is made out to be. Overheated eyes were cured by mixing the root of *matlal-xochitl* with mother's milk (note of warning: one suffering from this affliction would abstain from sex and wear on his neck a red crystal and on his right arm the eye of a fox). Bloodshot eyes, cataract, tumors in the eyes were all treated with plants that have been identified as having positive medicinal value. Catarrh and colds, common or otherwise, were helped by inhaling the odors of the plant *a-toch-ietl,* which is the pennyroyal of commercial medicine and is still used in some parts as a culicifuge.

Teeth, generally good, were often affected by swelling gums and toothache; the tooth was first punctured and a poultice made from the cactus *tenochtli* and farina then applied.

Tumors were cut out with obsidian knives, and after surgery the crushed leaves of a plant were applied. "Lameness of the hands" was to be cured by steeping the hands in warm water where the leaves of a bitter astringent had been crushed, after which the patient was to put his hand on an ant nest and "Let him patiently allow the lame hands to be bitten by the ants' pincers." Heart pains, burning of the

37. *The maguey plant* (metl) *and the method of gathering the sweet sap of the plant and storing it until it became fermented* octli.

heart, pains in the side, all of which came from overdrinking of the fermented *octli,* were treated with other herbs.

Stomach ailments were frequent among a people whose intestines swarmed with parasites; medicines to kill stomach worms, cures for tumors and dysentery appear often in the herbal. The bladderwort, which the Aztecs called *coanenepilli,* was used "when the flow of urine is shut off"; this was mixed with other bitter plants and "administered as an emetic." "If this medicine avails nothing," says the herbal, "it will be then necessary to take the pith of an extremely slender palm, covered with cotton, smeared with honey, and crushed with the herb *huihuitz-mallotic* and this cautiously inserted into the virile member."

Gout, rectal infections, rheumatism ("pain in the knees"), were frequent. More so were "cracks in the soles of the feet" for those who walked and had to carry burdens. There were remedies for "black blood" fevers (of which there is a good diagnosis in the herbals: "spit blood, body jerks and turns hither and thither, he sees little"). Hemorrhoids were present, and not, as often supposed, the result of modern occupational stresses; but if one had to go through the Aztec cure, perhaps it would be best to be left with the hemorrhoids ("before the cure, let him kill a weasel and eat it quite alone with dragon's blood"). Ringworm was endemic; the itch, dyspepsia, and warts were all part of the trouble of living. For all, specific cures were offered. Those who were "fear-burdened" had only to take a drink of the potion made of the herb called *tonatiuh-yxiuh* mixed with other plants and make a poultice of it with the blood of a wolf, the blood and excrement of an *acuecue-yxoyalotl,* ground together with sea foam.

Lice on the head, lousy distemper, and goatlike smell of the armpits could apparently be easily cured. There was much occupation with birth and many remedies were offered for recent parturition, to increase the flow of milk and for breast tubercles. The herbalist relieved pain in childbirth, but his methods would have appealed more to Jean Jacques Rousseau, who popularized the "noble savage," than to the gynecologist: "the womb of a woman entering childbirth is to be washed out with the juice of the plants. Into the womb you also inject the triturated herb *ayo nelhuatl* and eagle excrement. . . ."

There has been, to date, no comprehensive study of Aztec diseases. There is no evidence of surgery or of skull trepanning, as in Peru. However, this negative evidence is not decisive since we have few skeletal remains of these people. There is little doubt, however, that Aztec herbal medicine was far advanced. Certainly a people who could offer a remedy to relieve "the fatigue of those administering government and discharging public offices" * must have had a vast pharmacopeia or else a good sense of humor.

Yet there came a time, as it does to all, when medicines were of no help. From the time of a child's conception everyone in clan and tribe did his best to aid him through life; his mother was deflowered by others than the father so that evil, which was everywhere, would not harm him; at birth a priest had been called in to consult the auguries to be certain that the child was named on a lucky day; from cradle to fatal illness the fear of the "things" that moved through the supersensuous world never left him. What one did or did not do was only an attempt to steer successfully between Scylla and Charybdis on this uncertain sea of life. When the end approached, the dying must have felt that not enough had been done to propitiate the unseen powers, that perhaps somewhere along the way something had been forgotten, somewhere there had been a failure to conform.

Now that all had failed, the dying knew that the understanding alone was not enough to comprehend the world; somewhere the arguments of the heart must stand. The Aztec herbal gave final advice; the *ticitl,* "the cure doctor—will draw his auguries as to whether the patient is to die or get well from the eyes and nose. . . . A mark of death is a sootiness found in the middle of the eyes . . . eyes growing

---

* The bark of the tree *quetzal-ylin,* the flowers of *elo-xochitl* and *izqui-xochitl,* the almond with its fruit, which is the *tlapal-cacahuatl,* the flowers *cacalo-xochitl, huacal-xochitl, meca-xochitl, huey-nacaztli,* and all fine-smelling summer flowers, leaves of the trees *a-ylin, oyametl, ocotl, a-xocotl, eca-patli, tlaco-izqui-xochitl, quauh-yyauhtli, tomazquitl, ahuatl, tepeylin, ayauh-quahuitl,* and *te-papaquilti quahuitl,* flower-bearing plants with their shrubbery, which you gather before the wind rises—these are expressed one by one in clear spring water, into new vessels or vases. This then stays for a day and a night, when the *huitz-quahuitl* wood, with a red juice, is added as coloring.

Also the blood of wild animals, namely the red ocelot, *cuetlachtli, miztli, ocotochtli,* white ocelot, *tlaco-ocelotl,* is sought for. With this and the above liquors the body is well anointed.

These medicaments give gladiatorial strength to the body, drive fatigue far off, and also cast out timidity and strengthen the human heart.

Victor W. von Hagen

I   Temple of the Sun, Teotihuacán. Artificially raised, this pyramid became the standard method of displaying the dignity of the gods.

II   Calixtlahuaca, near Toluca. The highest temple in Mexico, at 9,517 feet, it is also one of the oldest. Its beginning is shrouded in mystery and is variously placed about A.D. 500.

Victor W. von Hagen

III   The frieze of arching jaguars and eagles at Tula, a temple-city of Toltec origin.

IV   A detail of the frieze of marching jaguars and eagles at the temple of Tula.

V   A detail of the wall of a serpent disgorging the skeleton of a man it has swallowed (Plate VI).

Victor W. von Hagen

VI   The outside wall of the temple at Tula. About it runs the *xical-coliuhqui*, the symbol of the Quetzalcoatl derived from the stylized head of the sky serpent.

VII   The figure of Chac-Mool, which first appeared at Tula, and then reappeared in Yucatán three centuries later. The hearts torn from sacrificial victims were said to have been thrown, as food for the gods, into the dish that the prone god holds on his stomach.

Andor Braun

VIII   The temple of Quetzalcoatl, Teotihuacán, with its dominant feathered serpent heads.

IX   A detail of a wall at Mitla, one of the best-known and best-preserved archaeological sites in Mexico. Its geometrical patterns seem inspired by and based on textile designs—"petrified weaving."

Victor W. von Hagen

X   Part of the North Plaza of Monte Albán, the present-day city of Oaxaca. It is surrounded by tall glyphed monoliths which, while not fully deciphered, suggest that they were set up during the occupation of the Mixtecs, the traditional border enemies of the Zapotecs, the first builders of the temple-city.

José Limón

XI   Gold breastplate from Monte Albán.

Victor W. von Hagen

XII   Xochicalco. A figure of a priest with plumed headdress sitting cross-legged. It highly suggests the Mayas in handling and could be mistaken for Maya.

XIII   Xochicalco. A view of the temple (north side), showing relative size of carving and temple.

Victor W. von Hagen

XIV   Aztec art. A vase
with a crouching figure, fashioned from the hard, brittle,
volcanic obsidian.

José Limón

XV   A rabbit, carv-
ed from a piece of
translucent quartz.

José Limón

XVI   The Totonacs, on
the coast of Vera Cruz
(where Cortés first landed),
produced a wide and varied
art: here is a clay Faustian
bearded figure, with lined
face, immense headgear.

José Limón

José Limón

XVII   An example of the curious original motifs in low relief on jade, from the Olmecs of Tabasco. The Olmecs are presumed to have been the cultural intermediaries between the Mayas and Central Mexico.

XVIII   The celebrated laughing heads, shaped, perhaps cast, from clay molds. These are typical of the Totonac area, but quite unique in all Mexico.

Victor W. von Hagen

dark and unseeing . . . nose getting thin. . . . Also ever
grinding of the teeth . . . and finally the babbling of words
without meaning . . . in the way of parrots. . . . You
may anoint the chest with pine wood crushed in water . . .
or puncture the skin with a wolf's bone or that of an eagle
or that of a puma . . . or you can hang close to the nostrils
the heart of a kestrel wrapped in a deerskin. . . . If none of
these avail, that fatal necessity is at hand . . . and death is
complete."

23. The Undead

"**I**T IS A FACT," someone says in Thomas Mann's *The Magic Mountain,* "that a man's dying is more the survivors' affair than his own"; it certainly was a fact to the Aztec. Death complicated everything. The survivors had to do penance in many ways for the unsocial act of their kinsman's dying. Does death put an end to us utterly and entirely? The Aztec did not know how to answer this. He did not have the subtlety of the French poet who answered the question of death by saying: *"Je suis, elle n'est pas; elle est, je ne suis plus."* "To the Aztec," writes Jacques Soustelle, "death and life were but aspects of the same reality." He could not (any more than you and I) imagine himself as not being.

Then came the "confession"—it is as ancient as man's society; the dying had to confess. It is a very important part of Christian ritual and communistic political behavior patterns; it goes back to a far-reaching primitivity. Confessions had a virture of their own; they were essential to neutralize the evil influences brought on by dying. For example, the Aztec believed that the act of dying caused uncleanliness, for dying was a form of social defilement. There actually existed a mystic bond between the dying man and death, some sort of participation like that which unites a living man and his belongings. Man is responsible; he is the silent accomplice of the evil which is being propagated. He must confess.

The sorcerer was called in to attend to it. He arrived, consulted the sacred roll, and tobacco smoke was blown across the dying man; invocations were made to the gods so that he would die like an Aztec of good sense. Then they prepared the body for burial. First in his mouth a greenstone to take the place of his heart. It was not like the obolus which the Greeks put into the mouth of the dead to pay the passage across the river Styx; rather it was a heart symbol—

the "Heart of Jade"—for his journey to the unworld. Food was prepared, drink put in bowls, and the mummy bundle made complete. The next step was inhumation. Two courses were open to the Aztecs for the disposal of the dead, but the choice really depended on social position. If he was a common Indian, the body was swathed in cloth, tied with a cord, and festooned with paper flags; funeral chants (*miccacuicatl*) were put into the mouths of the dead by the living:

> *Where shall I go?*
> *Where shall I go?*
> *The road of the god of duality.*
> *Is your house perchance in the place of the fleshless?*
> *Perchance inside heaven?*
> *or here on earth only*
> *is the place of the fleshless?*

Death stirs both primitive and civilized, for to die, at least to the Aztec, was to accomplish an act of incalculably far-reaching potentialities. The dead were in reality living: they had merely passed from one phase to another; they were invisible, impalpable, invulnerable. The dead, or, better, in their feeling, the *undead*, had become the unseen members of the clan. The body of the common man, swathed in cloth, tied into a death bundle, had things of his life and other things for his death-life journey. He was then cremated and the ashes were put into a pot on which the piece of jade was placed, the pot being kept in the house.

Cremation was general except where those of elevated rank were concerned; the leaders were entombed. The "Anonymous Conqueror" found one of them after the rape of Mexico-Tenochtitlán. He found a mummy sitting with his personal device, sword, and jewels amounting to "three thousand castellanos."

The departed went to those tutelary genii who had protected them in life; the knights of the Eagle, warriors, and valiant women (considered the same as warriors) went to the land of Tlaloc, the rain god; he also cordially received those souls who died by drowning, since he was the god of water. How one acted or did not act in life had no relation to one's degree of immortality; conduct in life did not determine the soul's place in the shades. "The vertical world," says Dr. Vaillant, "was divided into heavens and hells [there were thirteen heavens and nine hells] which had no moral significance." It was one's occupation in life and manner of dying that determined it: warriors went to the eastern paradise, flower-filled; women who died in childbirth went into a western paradise and came to earth to haunt children and women in unspent spleen. Those of the undead who were unclassified made the passage to Mictlán; this was a veritable *via dolorosa:* rivers to cross, mountains to climb, deserts to cross, enduring of freezing winds and rains; the dead had full need of all the charms that the survivors put into the funeral pyre as talismans for the journey. When the soul arrived at the realm of the Lord of the Dead, he was assigned to one of the nine hells; the piece of greenstone tied to the mouth when the cadaver was swathed was left as a pledge in the seventh hell.

Poor human beings, we must needs furnish ourselves with illusions even in death. Since man, primitive or civilized, cannot endure the idea of a mechanistic interpretation of the universe, he cannot grasp the fact that when one is not, one ceases to be. Ignorance is not alone a necessary condition of happiness, it is a condition of life itself; the sentiments that make life bearable to all spring out of falsehoods and are fed on illusions.

"We do not believe," said the Aztecs, "we fear."

Meanwhile, the living must go into mourning for eighty days. There were a variety of impositions and taboos on food, dress, and indulgence in sex; sustenance had to be regularly placed at the death urn, prayers given, blood offered from cuts made in the ears and tongue. All must be done to obtain the good will of the recent dead; their displeasure could have dire consequences and could expose the living to twofold retribution: from the justly offended recently dead and from fellow clan members, who collectively would have to suffer the consequences of the dead's anger. After eighty days the taboo was lifted. It was repeated on and off for four years: "For . . . it is a fact that a man's dying is more the survivors' affair than his own."

Such, from womb to tomb, was the daily life of the Aztec common man, base of the pyramid of Aztec society. Higher up in rank by election there were the clan heads; these in turn had representation on the tribal council (*tecuhtli*), and at the top of this curious *mélange* of elected officials were the "council of four" (*tlatoani*). Finally, at the apex was the semidivine Chief Speaker, the Uei Tlatoani, head of the army, high priest, the court of last appeal in the city-state of Tenochtitlán.

The well-remembered "king" Moctezuma was the Uei Tla-toani in that fateful year of 1519.

38. *Moctezuma Xocoyotzin—Moctezuma II, the Younger (reigned 1503–20). As Chief Speaker he ruled Mexico when it reached its apogee. Although the materials of his clothes were finer, basically they were the same style as his subjects: cloak, breechclout, and sandals. The headgear is his "crown."*

III

The Aztec 'Kings' and the Directing Classes

24. Moctezuma

THE RULER of the Aztecs had as title "One Who Speaks" (derived from the verb *tlatoa*, "to speak"); he was elected. So William Prescott was not entirely incorrect in calling their form of government an "elective monarchy." The leader was not absolute, as in the Peruvian theocracy—he did not claim ownership of the land, the earth, the people, as did the Inca—the Aztecs were in theory democratic.[81] Each family was a member of a soil community; a cluster of these families formed a clan, of which twenty made up the tribe of the Tenochas. Each clan had its own council and an elected leader; of these the oldest or wisest or more experienced were selected to make up an interclan council, the link between the clans and the tribe's governing body. This council was narrowed down to four principals, who were advisers to the leader of state and, as well, electors of the "king" (functioning, to pursue a convenient analogy, as did the electors of the Holy Roman Empire), since "kings" were not such by primogeniture but could be selected by the *tlatoani* from the brothers of the previous ruler, or, if he had none, from his nephews. These *tlatoani* were the key figures in Aztec government; they chose that "noble" descendant who in their mind was most distinguished in valor, war, knowledge. Such a one was Moctezuma, who was "crowned" in 1503. There is a description of him which is the most penetrating we have of any such ruler of any of the Sun Kingdoms of ancient America.

It was November 8, 1519, when Hernán Cortés arrived with his small army at Tenochtitlán. Where two causeways coalesced, "Here nearly one thousand of the chief citizens came out to greet me, all dressed alike and richly; on coming to speak with me each performed a ceremony very common to them, to wit, placing his hand on the ground and then kissing it, so that for nearly an hour I stood while they performed this ceremony.

"Moctezuma himself came out to meet us with some two hundred nobles. . . . They came forward in two long lines keeping close to the walls of the street. . . . Moctezuma was borne along in the middle of the street with two lords, one on his right and left. . . . Moctezuma wore sandles, whereas the others were barefoot."

Bernal Díaz, who did not have to content himself with lofty political remarks, kept to description where Cortés left off. "The Great Moctezuma was about forty years old, of good height and well proportioned, slender and spare of flesh, not very swarthy, but of the natural colour and shade of an Indian. He did not wear his hair long . . . his scanty beard was well shaped and thin. His face was somewhat long, but cheerful . . . He was very neat and clean and bathed once every day in the afternoon. He had many women as mistresses, daughters of Chieftains, and he had two great Cacicas as his legitimate wives. He was free from unnatural offences [i.e., sodomy]. The clothes that he wore one day, he did not put on again until four days later [the Lord-Inca never wore the same garment twice]. He had two hundred Chieftains in his guard . . . and when they went to speak to him they were obliged to take off their rich mantles and put on others of little worth . . . to enter barefoot with their eyes lowered to the ground, and not to look up in his face. . . . And they made him three obeisances . . ." (The Lord-Inca imposed a similar ritual.)

Moctezuma ate like a grand vizier. "For each meal over thirty different dishes were prepared . . . and they placed small pottery braziers beneath the dishes so that they should not get cold . . . he had such a variety of dishes . . . turkeys, pheasants, native partridges, quail, tame and wild ducks, venison, wild boar, reed birds, pigeons, hares . . . so numerous that I cannot finish naming them . . ." Moctezuma sat "on a low stool, soft and richly worked . . . Four very beautiful cleanly women brought water for his hands in a sort of deep basin which they call *xicales* . . . And two other women brought him tortilla bread, and as soon as he began to eat they placed before him a sort of wooden screen painted over with gold, so that no one should watch him eating. . . . four great chieftains [these were the *tlatoani*] who were old men came and stood beside [the women] and with these Moctezuma now and then conversed . . . They say that these elders were his near relations, and were his counsellors . . . They brought him fruit of all the different kinds . . . From time to time in cup-shaped vessels of pure gold, a certain drink made from cacao [was served]. . . . Sometimes at meal-times there were present some very ugly humpbacks . . . who are their jesters, and other Indians, who must have been buffoons . . .

"There were also placed on the table three tubes much painted and gilded, which held *liquidambar* mixed with certain herbs which they call *tabaco*, and when he had finished eating . . . he inhaled the smoke from one of those tubes . . . with that he fell asleep."

Moctezuma became a demigod. Although elected, with leadership he took on semidivinity. He was high priest, supreme commander of the army, and head of state, a plenary ruler, advised by council, with his power only held in check by ancient mores. Moctezuma was the ninth in succession, the nephew of the last ruler, Ahuitzotl, and grandson of Moctezuma I (surnamed "the Wrathy"). As an Aztec ruler-aspirant he was trained like all such in the "religious" schools, the *calmecac* ("house of the large corridors"). There, with the image of Quetzalcoatl painted on the wall, he learned by means of glyphic charts the history of the Tenochas. He was taught to read glyph writing, to remember the list of dates of rulers and history, which succinctly was:

Aztec history begins	A.D. 1168
Tenochtitlán settled	A.D. 1325

List of Aztec realm leaders after A.D. 1375:

Acamapichtli	ruled 1375–1395	Moctezuma I	ruled	1440–1469
Huitzilhuitl	" 1395–1414	Axayacatl	"	1469–1481
Chimalpopoca	" 1414–1428	Tizoc	"	1481–1486
Itzcoatl	" 1428–1440	Ahuitzotl	"	1486–1503
	Moctezuma II ruled 1503–1520			

He studied the use of Aztec arms, swords, slings, and arrows, for it was expected he would be a military leader; once he knew and understood ideographic writing he learned

about the stars, astrology, the calendar, and through constant
reading of the *tonalamatl* (used as an aid in memory) he
learned the rituals and interpretation of phenomena. As a
youth Moctezuma had taken a very active part in the wars;
later he devoted much attention to religion, "scrupulous in
his attentions to all the burdensome ceremonial of the Aztec
worship." José de Acosta also said that he was "grave and
staid and spake little, so when hee gave his opinion . . . then
he was feared and respected. . . . Hee marched with such
gravitie . . . they all sayd the name of Moctezuma ['Coura-
geous Lord'] agreed very well with his nature."

When elected, Moctezuma was found sweeping down the
133 steps of the great Temple of Huitzilopochtli ("to show
that he desired not the Emprey," adds Acosta in an aside).
"The electors . . . giving him notice that hee was chosen king
. . . he was ledde before the harth of their gods . . . where he
offered sacrifice in drawing blood from his eares & the calves
of his legges."

First, war, where he went in person to an enterprise "necessary for his coronation," [1] i.e., prisoners for sacrifice. He
moved down to the Gulf, extended Aztec domination in both
directions, and returned in triumph to Mexico and had his
nose septum pierced for insertion of the royal emerald for
his coronation. The number of sacrificial victims did not
quite reach that of his uncle's piety; Ahuitzotl had immolated twelve thousand.

Moctezuma was "crowned" with a sort of miter; the color
symbol of his power was blue-green. Immediately after coming
to power he turned out the rankless people about him, com-
manding that "only the most noble and most famous men of
his realme shoulde live within his pallace," thus severing
the democratic base of Chief Speaker; it had been "custome"
to have people of all shades and hues about the royal rooms
ever since the time of "king" Itzcoatl, who had been born of
a slave concubine in his father's house. Moctezuma seems to
have taken on some of the prerogatives of a god; whether
this was done before him by other Chief Speakers is not made
clear.

Dress for Moctezuma was as the lower man's except that
it was more elaborate. He wore the breechclout, elaborate
sandals, the manta (*tilmantli*), and all the other accouter-
ments so highly praised by the conquerors. These descriptions by the Spaniards, which were later dismissed by eighteenth-century historians as inspired by the heady fumes of
war, have been confirmed by archaeology. Few—outside of

the Maya kingdom—lived as sumptuously; the apparent over-drawing is no exaggeration of the real splendor of it all.

Marriage for the "first gentleman of the realm" was basically no different from the tying of the *tilmantli* among the lower orders, but, like royal marriages everywhere, it was often an alliance. There was one legitimate wife (although Bernal Díaz says two); the Spanish historian Oviedo elicited from Doña Isabel, one of the legitimate daughters of Moctezuma, that he had 150 children by his various concubines, but con-firmed that he had only one legitimate wife. She was the executive; all others took orders from her. Indeed, our terms "legitimate" and "illegitimate" had no meaning.

The numerous progeny were trained for office. This is true of all polygamous marriages; the Inca used his enormous offspring as sources for leadership in the realm and the Aztec practiced a similar nepotism. Nezahualpilli, "king" of Tex-coco, allied to Mexico, "had more than two thousand con-cubines." [81] In a society where war took men's lives faster than they could be created by simple monogamous birth, polygyny seemed most functional. Besides nothing so favors a marriage and consequently social stability as the indulgence of temporary polygamy.

Moctezuma ruled well. He spread the realm farther than all others before him; tribute was collected from 371 towns; justice in particular was well organized by him. "If there were any excesse of defect he did then punish it rigorously. . . . And also to discern how his ministers did execute their officers he often disguised himselfe . . . if they offended, they were punished. Besides that he was a great justicier and very noble, he was very valiant and happy . . . and he ob-tained great victories and came to his greatness." [1] But the times were out of joint: the heavens and the hells rose to plague him. What we would call natural phenomena, to them was evil omen: it snowed in Mexico; the volcano Popocaté-petl, which had lain quiescent for a long time, became active. A child was born with two heads; the "king" of Texcoco (he of the two thousand women), who was a "greate Magitian," came over one day "at an extraordinary hour" to tell him that the gods had revealed he would lose his whole realm. To give it all a sense of history, Quetzalcoatl, who had de-clared against human sacrifice and was the cultural hero of these lands, had sailed away in exile into the Atlantic saying that he would again return in the same year of his birth to "re-establish my rule." His birth had been in the Aztec year of 1-Reed (Ce-Acatl); in the Aztec calendar this fell in the

years 1363, 1467—and 1519. For years Moctezuma had all
but given up the military direction of his government and
was surrounded by a corps of astrologers, augurs, necro-
mancers, and mediums from whom he sought, by the
interpretation of signs, symbols, and observation of the portents, to learn what to do to win back the favor of the gods.

What had happened was simple enough: white men had
reached America's shores. In 1502, one year before Moctezuma's coronation, Cristóbal Colón, on his fourth and last
voyage, had made contact with the Mayas; it did not take
long for this event to boil over from the Maya councils and be
carried over the trails from people to market and from tribe
to tribe. Later, Yañez Pinzón and Juan Díaz de Solís skirted
the shores of Yucatán, and once again rumor sniffed the
breeze, as it were, traveled over the jungles, and somewhere
was set down by a glyph writer to be sent to Moctezuma:
strange bearded men in large boats have come from out of the
ocean-sea.

No "king" in Aztec history had so terrible a problem to
cope with as Moctezuma.

25. The Function of Tenochtitlán

THE RULE and organization of Tenochtitlán was activated through the system already outlined: the "king," Uei Tlatoani, gave his desires to the "council of four"; they in turn conveyed it to the larger body of clan heads (*tecuhtli*), then down to the clan body, where another official, who enforced peace and was the clan leader during a war, gave to members of the clan the programs promulgated from the higher reaches.

This clan, the basic unit of the system, enforced clan peace, organized for war, rounded out clan taxation; orders through these methods reached down to the very last rung of the social ladder. It seems that the Aztecs did not administer the affairs of conquered peoples. Perhaps they were not interested in doing so. The Incas in Peru had a system of sending *mitimaes*, a "safe" population of Quechua-speaking peoples, into newly conquered lands and removing the unsafe of the newly conquered. By this system the Incas conquered and amalgamated that which they conquered. The Aztecs had no such system. They imposed a tribute, not excessive, except for sacrificial victims, a contribution which fitted into the conquerors' economy. This was brought every six months to Tenochtitlán. Still the Aztecs won no friends and forged no empire. They went through all the social evolution of Neolithic states everywhere: they moved from the land, where at first all worked at agriculture, to the city which became a temple-city, where a social surplus produced nonfarmers—specialists in architecture, and sculpture, lapidaries, and priest-craftsmen, people who themselves no longer grew food. Then their society passed into the city-state with satellite towns, and Tenochtitlán developed an extended priestly class who exacted "first fruits" for the temples. Then lastly it became the conquering and finally the tribute city.

There were enough reasons for this. The Aztecs were fighting people. They had no luxuries on their land: cotton, brilliant bird feathers, chocolate, gold, rubber were not of their earth's bounty. If they wanted these things, they got them by conquest. Moreover as they became specialized they manufactured and traded. It was difficult enough: each region was hostile to every other; there were few natural avenues; imbroglios had to be called off so trading could be carried on. There was a great lack of unity even among towns nominally Aztec. As Tenochtitlán, the conquering city, widened its horizons, new products, new ideas came into it, and gradually luxuries were converted into necessities.

Trade became vital to Mexico. And war was continuous; tribute, the result of conquest, poured in from many far-flung places and was distributed among the clans. As this gave people more leisure from the fields, leisure was devoted to manufacture, which in turn produced articles they traded for luxuries at the market. A new class of merchant (*pochteca*) came into being—a phenomenon in ancient America— traders who had their own guilds, their own gods, and were above the laws that applied to most. They set out from Mexico periodically with long trains of human carriers (*tamenes*), sixty pounds on their backs, preceded by the lordly *pochteca*. Protected in disputed terrain by soldiers, the human caravans penetrated into southern Mexico, into and beyond Guatemala, down as far as Nicaragua. They traded Aztec manufactured goods for the raw products of the hotlands: emeralds, which slowly found their way from Muzo in Colombia (the only place they were found in pre-Hispanic America), gold from Panama, feathers from Guatemala, jaguar skins, eagle feathers, cotton, chocolate, chicle, rubber, live birds for the royal aviary in Mexico (the source of plumage for the feather weavers). Roads of a sort were opened; Aztec garrisons were placed at strategic places or among the newly conquered. The *pochteca* moved freely.

There is a natural limit to conquest. The Aztecs had no definite plan of assimilation. Conquest often followed trade as the Aztecs got information on riches and defenses brought back by the merchants; sometimes the process went the other way: villages, city-states, subjected to sharp wars of conquest, were made to yield tribute. The number of these expanded until at the time of Moctezuma there were 371.

So during the growth of Aztec power all the riches of all these cultures were pouring into their capital.

Mexico-Tenochtitlán was an island and a watery city. It was something like Venice. There were the same type of

39. *Mexico-Tenochtitlán as it would have appeared to an Aztec artist. There were the same type of* calli *and* campi *as in Venice, with canals, bridges, and dikes. The plan is schematic, but seen in the center is the great temple, the* teocalli; *about it was the main plaza. To the north was Tlaltelolco, a rival city, until it was subjugated by swift conquest and made a part of greater Mexico.*

calli and *campi*, with hundreds of meandering streets, filled with canals, bridges, and dikes. This Tenochtitlán began, as Venice, not out of "feelings of men" who founded cities, but out of safety. Just as the primitive Venetians took possession of the tide-washed sandbanks in the Adriatic and turned this undefined swampy tract into a city with its canals and waterways, so did the Aztecs, fleeing the mainland, seek safety on the two marsh-bound islets three miles from shore on Lake Texcoco.

Tenochtitlán was named after a cactus, *tenochtli*, which grew on the islet; the people became the Tenocha, the city Tenochtitlán. The name broken into radicals shows its origin: *tetl*, "rock," *nochtli*, "cactus," *tlán*, "place of." An eagle is supposed to have perched on the cactus during the founding; however, one of the Ten who, according to legend, founded the city was called "Tenoch"; it could be that this gave the city its name.

The oval-shaped valley of Anáhuac at 7,244 feet altitude, 30 by 50 miles, held the waters of the lakes, which were identified by five separate names although they formed a continuous body of water that varied from fresh to saline. The largest of the lakes was Texcoco. Directly out from Chapultepec forest, three miles more or less ("seven leagues" said Hernán Cortés), there were two islets, rock outcrops surrounded by mudbanks and reed-fringed. This was the base of Tenochtitlán.

The first buildings were structures of wattle and daub, the "immortal" house even today of the upland peasant. Then followed the temple, which, rebuilt from century to century, grew into the awesome Temple of Huitzilopochtli (the present site of Mexico's Cathedral). While developing the two islets * the Aztecs apparently maintained by treaty some foothold for cultivation on the mainland, augmenting this by the ingenious *chinampa*, the "floating garden," and the space between these formed the canals. Centuries of these operations enlarged the original mud flats until "Greater Mexico-Tenochtitlán," that is, Tenochtitlán and Tlaltelolco, formed

---

* There were two islets; one, Tlaltelolco, had been occupied by Aztec warriors coming over from adjacent Atzacoalco on the mainland; Tenochtitlán was settled by those coming from Chapultepec. The two grew up rivals like Buda and Pest or Minneapolis and St. Paul. A bridge connected them. Rivalry led to war in 1473; Tlaltelolco was conquered and incorporated into Greater Mexico.

a city 1¾ miles square and containing upwards of 2,500 acres. This was a sizable area: Rome's walls at the time of Marcus Aurelius enclosed a city of only 3,500 acres; London town in the time of Samuel Pepys was scarcely any larger.

Mexico-Tenochtitlán as a city grew as Venice grew: the Aztec raided the land about the lakes—a conquest here, a land treaty there—until by A.D. 1400 most of the city-states and their lands were under Aztec domination. Their safety assured, they began to build the great causeways that connected the island kingdom to the mainland. There were four; the best and most authentic description of them is by Hernán Cortés, the man who destroyed the city.

"The great city of Tenochtitlán . . . is two leagues [five miles] . . . to any point on the mainland. Four causeways lead to it . . . some twelve feet wide." The one which he took to enter the city in 1519 began at Ixtapalapa (". . . we saw so many cities and villages built in the water and other great towns on dry land and that straight and level Causeway going towards Mexico . . ." says Bernal Díaz). This causeway ("as broad as two lances and broad enough for eight horsemen to ride abreast") went for about a mile and there made junction with another causeway coming from the city of Coyoacán. Here there was a fort with battlements and a drawbridge; then the causeway went on some two miles directly north to the city. It was much used, "but broad as it is, it was so crowded with people that there was hardly room for them all . . ." [25] The second was an auxiliary causeway with aqueduct, which arched in a curve connected with some part of the mainland and entered this main causeway close to the entrance of the city. The third went westward toward Chapultepec (branching off to Tlacopán), i.e., Tacuba. This carried the aqueduct to the heart of the city. "Along . . . [this] causeway two pipes are constructed of masonry, each two paces broad [6 feet] and about as high as a man; one of which conveys a stream of water very clear and fresh." The other one lay empty to be used when the first was being cleaned. As the causeway had at intervals removable bridges in case of attack, the fresh water conduit, as explained by Hernán Cortés, "flows into a kind of [ceramic] trough as thick as an ox [twenty-five-inch conduit], which occupies the whole of the bridge." * The fourth and last cause-

* There were two aqueducts: one built by Ahuitzol (reigned 1486–1503), which went from Coyoacán over the arched causeway; it also emptied into a fountain in the main square.

way, the shortest, not much over a half-mile in length, connected the city with the mainland at Tepeaca.

This system of causeways, the greatest engineering feat of the Aztecs, had a twofold purpose: to facilitate communication and to serve as a dike or levee. The lakes were subject to rise and fall; rain could raise the level rapidly (there was no outlet); wind could raise huge waves that lapped up to and over the city, which was subject to frequent inundations (as it is still today). Since Tenochtitlán had almost been destroyed by flood in 1440, the then reigning Moctezuma I applied to his friend and ally, the ruler of the advanced city-state of Texcoco. The system of causeway dikes was constructed in such a fashion as to contain the waters of Lake Xochimilco. Moreover, by breaking up the lakes with other causeway dikes, the freshness of Xochimilco's water was preserved and Mexico-Tenochtitlán was protected from the rise of the water level. As much of the lake was shallow (six feet), the causeways were doubtless first pontooned and later replaced with *chinampas* firmly anchored to the shallows. With all their records the Aztecs left us nothing illustrating their one great engineering feat.

The city, like Cuzco, capital of the Incas in Peru, was divided into four sections, corresponding to the causeways, which entered the city from three of the four cardinal directions. Each formal entrance to the city proper had a roadblock, where taxes were collected.

After the street ceased to be a causeway, the view along it was clear and unobstructed ("one can see from one end to the other, though it is some two miles in length"), and both sides of the streets were lined with houses ("very beautiful, very large, both private dwellings and temples"). House styles varied with the rank of the owner. Those of the lower class were constructed with walls of wattle and smeared with mud, grass-thatched; those of rank were raised on a stone platform (in case of flood), made of sun-dried brick, plastered over, and brilliantly colored.

The ordinary house, invariably one-storied and with a pitched straw roof, had its postern to the street, a patio garden within, and by a narrow canal, which was its street, was the entrance. There was also a jetty for the dugout canoe. The principal houses were two-storied, made of *tezontli* stone, with flat roofs. The city "had many wide and handsome streets," said the "Anonymous Conqueror"; they were in all probability of adobe, since to him they were "formed half of hard earth like a brick pavement." Many if not most of these "streets" were waterways, canals such as in Venice; "there are principal streets, entirely of water which can only be traversed by canoes." [3] Each dwelling had a small plot of earth, a garden; this is evident in the fragment of an Aztec map (made circa 1480) drawn on *amatl* paper and showing very clearly the individual houses, ground plots, streets, and the great waterways.

Tenochtitlán was divided into twenty sections (*calpulli*). These the Spaniards called *barrios* (wards); we refer to them as clans. Each clan had its own *teocalli* (*temple*) and its school, each *calpulli* its name and emblem (coat of arms). In the largest of the squares was the great pyramid to Huitzilopochtli and Tlaloc. The 200-foot-high structure was double-stepped and double-templed. The temple on the left, painted white and blue, was to the national god, the Hummingbird Wizard; the other, white with blood-red background, was that of the rain god and it very much impressed the Spanish. "It is one," wrote Hernán Cortés, "whose size and magnitude no human tongue can describe" although Padre Acosta tried to do so: "Upon the toppe of the Temple were two . . . Chappells and in them were two Idolls." The structures rested on a forty-foot square, for the pyramids, like all in Mexico, were truncated. Bernal Díaz ascended the great pyramid and counted the steps—114 within the temples, where Cortés and Moctezuma had their famous discourse on the value of gods. The roof beams and the stone were beautifully worked. It was so sacrosanct that few could enter, and when Cortés wanted to dislodge them and plant a cross in their stead, Moctezuma cut short the visit, saying "he had to pray and offer certain sacrifices on account of the great *tatacul*, that is to say, sin, which he had committed in allowing us to ascend his great Cue . . ." [25] Near to the steps was the large sacrificial stone; Bernal Díaz shuddered to think of it: ["Here] they put the poor Indians for sacrifice, there was a bulky image like a dragon . . . and much blood . . ." *

---

* Bernal Díaz described the view from the top of that "huge and cursed temple": ". . . we saw three causeways . . . that is the causeway of Iztapalapa by which we had entered Mexico . . . Tacuba, and that of Tepeaquilla, and we saw the fresh water that comes from Chapultepec [over the Tlacopán-Tacuba causeway] . . . we saw the bridges . . . we saw . . . the Cues [temples] and oratories like towers and fortresses and all gleaming white, and it was a wonderful thing to behold; then the houses with flat roofs . . ."

The stone-paved great plaza measured, as do the boundaries of the *zócalo* of present-day Mexico, 520 by 600 feet, and within that square there was the great *teocalli,* with four lesser pyramids on its several sides: the Temple of Quetzalcoatl, a rounded structure entwined with green, open-fanged serpents; a raised dais on which gladiators fought; the sacred ball court, with, on one side, the residence of the officiating priests and, on the other, the house of the military order of the Eagle, an elite warrior class. The *tzompantli,* or skull rack, on which hung the craniums of the sacrificial victims, was close to the ball court. Three causeways terminated in the main square (just as in Cuzco, the capital of the Incas, the roads of "four quarters" that ran the length and breadth of their land terminated or began in the main plaza); of these, Ixtapalapa was the southern road and the causeway by which the Spanish made their entry. The water entered the city at the great square and was from there either piped off to other sections or was collected in water jugs, as one still sees women today collect it. The city, gleaming white in the sun, with barbarically colored houses and temples, surrounded by the blue lake, must have appeared to be a floating city, something out of *The Thousand and One Nights,* with its gardens and aviaries and multitudes of people, giving it a life as orderly as a termitarium; and so it seemed to Bernal Díaz: "We were amazed and said it was like the enchantments they tell of in the legend of Amadis." The impression that the city made was so lasting that even when this same Bernal Díaz was eighty-four years old, half blind, half deaf, aching from the old wounds and having nothing for all his time and effort, he could still write: "It was indeed wonderful, and, now that I am writing about it, it all comes before my eyes as though it had happened but yesterday."

The other half of the great square, empty of buildings, was the market (*tiaquiz*). Here the people were addressed by the directing classes. At one end was the sacred stone of war where the captains met before going off to do battle; at the other end was the calendar stone. In front of this was the new palace of Moctezuma. It was an immense structure, as large in area as the plaza, a virtual city in itself (the nineteenth-century modern Ayuntamiento occupies the same area today); it repeated the features of the great square in miniature. Two stories in height, Moctezuma's living quarters were on the second floor. The rest of the magnificent structure was honeycombed with rooms. There were sumptuous quarters for the "kings" of the city-states of Texcoco and Tlacopán, to which the Aztecs were allied. There were other rooms for at least three hundred accompanying guests, always coming and going. Below there were the tribunal rooms, especially for those held until given trial, rooms for the "judges" (*achcauhcalli*), the public repository (*petalcalco*) where all the tribute from the 371 tribute towns was delivered and stored for distribution. It is to one of these rooms that Bernal Díaz was conducted to see the tribute: ". . . his steward was a great Cacique . . . and he kept the acounts of all the revenue that was brought to Montezuma . . . Montezuma had two houses full of every sort of arms . . . and in other quarters, cotton, foodstuffs, chocolate, feathers, gold, jewels, all that was part of the tribute-economy." In other sections were the rooms of the administrators who kept record of the economy of the theodemocracy.

On the second floor were the rooms of Moctezuma's wife, his 150 concubines and their offspring, his hundreds of guards and attendants. "Every morning at dawn," said Cortés, "there were over six hundred nobles and chief men present in his palace, some of whom were seated, others walking around the rooms. . . . The servants of these nobles filled two or three courtyards and overflowed into the street."

The rooms were decorated amazingly with carved cedar beams which "could not be bettered anywhere," said stout Cortés, "for they were cut with ornamental borders of flowers, birds and fish." The walls were presumably adorned with hangings. Bernal Díaz and his "merrie boyes" were lodged in the Palace of Axayacatl, near to Moctezuma's palace on the square, "where there were great halls and chambers canopied with the cloth of the country . . . [the walls] coated with shining cement and swept and garlanded." Moctezuma's was decorated with murals and bas-reliefs, with door hangings and so many rooms and doors that the "halls of Montezuma" seemed like a labyrinth, at least to Díaz, who confessed: "I entered it more than four times, and there was always more and more to see and always I grew weary from walking and for this I was never able to see everything."

Attached to the palace, or within it (for it was full of patios), was the royal aviary. This astounded the conquistadors, for there were no zoos in Europe—they were unheard of. "There were ten pools of water in which they kept every kind of waterfowl known in these parts . . . and I can vouch for it to Your Majesty," wrote Cortés to Charles V, fearful that if he described such a thing as an aviary the king would think him mad, "I can vouch that these birds, who only eat fish, receive some 250 pounds daily."

How large was the city, how large the fief of the city-state of Tenochtitlán? No one knew. Cortés admitted that he was "unable to find out the exact extent of . . . the kingdom." He thought it "as large as Spain." Certainly, even taking natural exaggeration into account, it was one of the world's largest cities; few of the temple-cities in the Old World seem to have been as large.

Of course it was not unique; ". . . a very unusual conjunction of circumstances," said V. Gordon Childe, "which occurred at most five times—in the Tigris-Euphrates delta, in the Nile Valley, in the Indus Basin, in Mexico, Central America, and . . . Peru." Neolithic peoples depended wholly on agriculture, went through what he has called "the Urban Revolution," changed their social structure radically, both psychologically and economically, by intensifying the exploitation of the land, creating social surplus, freeing many from agricultural work, and creating the full-time specialist. The city with all its complexities was the result. People crowding into cities was a radical departure from the "American pattern," where, either because of a basically unsocial nature or because of the extravagant methods of Neolithic cultivation (vast tracts of land were needed), clans or families were separated by considerable distances and only came together when the need was general.

How populous was ancient Tenochtitlán? The conquistadors said there were from seventy to a hundred thousand inhabited houses on the island kingdom; if each house had between four and ten inhabitants, averaging six to the house, the population would have been about one half million. Cortés's small army of one thousand men, even with his Indian auxiliaries, could not have beaten down *that* number. "Read eight thousand instead of eighty thousand houses," said Juan de Rivera, who—though he cheated at cards, tried to rob Cortés, and, to top it all, was cross-eyed—was nevertheless a keen observer and doubted the figures; so did Bernal Díaz. One historian gives thirty thousand for Mexico-Tenochtitlán,[94] but a modern French authority often quoted in this book falls back on the old figures; he says that the city had "a population certainly more than five hundred thousand and probably inferior to one million." [74]

The population of a historyless people is like the metaphysics of finance: it depends on how one reads the statistics.

Hernán Cortés should have known; he was a battle commander, and, while he padded his figures (as all commanders do), he had to have "an estimate of the situation"; of the population of Mexico he says flatly that Texcoco, one of the largest and most cultivated of the city-states on the mainland facing the city, "must contain some thirty thousand inhabitants"; double that sum, be utterly reckless and triple it, Mexico-Tenochtitlán had no more than ninety thousand inhabitants. Even "reduced" it was still one of the largest cities in the world: at that time London had no more than forty thousand, Paris could boast sixty-five thousand.

Although the Aztecs were not an empire (as the Incas were an empire), although they did not have what most regard as the essential elements of civilization—metal, the wheel, draft animals, the rotary quern—they had a form of organization, an intensification of older native techniques, which made possible the achievements that follow and stamped indelibly all things they touched with the word "Mexican."

IV

The Achievements

26. What Mexico Wrought

AZTEC ARCHITECTURE perished with the Conquest. We can mingle our tears with those of Hernán Cortés on that day of Saint Hippolytus, August 13, 1521, when Mexico-Tenochtitlán, ". . . one of the most beautiful sights in the world," was utterly destroyed in the process of being taken. With its collapse there was a complete loss of the scale and purpose of its architecture. What was left after the holocaust of conquest were the remains of temples and pyramids adorned with names which jingle like ponderous, brassy tassels, and not much more. Nothing has been left of the common houses, not even a ground plan to give an idea of how they were served by their architecture. However, from the existing codices, archaeological excavations, and descriptions by the destroyers, and by means of theoretical reconstruction, we know this: "Public buildings, of a secular character, like the clan or the chief's quarters, were large-scale projections of the domestic architecture." Dr. Vaillant develops this theme: "The addition of many apartments for attendants and concubines, a swimming pool and a menagerie, such as composed the palace of Montezuma, did not alter structurally or in basic plan the scheme of rectangular rooms set about a patio"—which was the home of the common Indian.

Most of Aztec architecture lay about the immediate vicinity of the lakes, dotted like satellites around Tenochtitlán. It is all gone. Yet enough has been found in the descriptive literature developed out of archaeology to attempt its reconstruction.

Tenochtitlán appears to have had one of the best planned urban centers of all ancient American cultures. It had not, to be sure, the mechanistic perfection of Cuzco, capital of the Incas, but its attention to human comfort for all the population, its zeal in transporting water through aqueducts, its hedonistic approach to life—often absent in the austere Inca city—doubtless surpassed all others. The only city-state to which it can be compared, where much of this luxuriousness obtained, was that of Chan-Chan, capital of the Chimú Empire in the desert coast of Peru and contemporaneous with the Aztec capital.

Beyond all else the thought of God is an incitement. Religion was the dominating factor in Aztec life and Tenochtitlán was "divine." The whole of it was, in its essence, religious; everything important within it was dedicated, in one form or another, to religion.

The symbol of it was the pyramid. The great *teocalli* stood in the plaza encircled by a high wall fashioned as writhing snakes, and hence its name, *coatepantli*. It measured at its base 150 by 150 feet and rose to about 160 feet high at its truncated apex, which was 70 feet square; on it rested two temples dedicated to the principal gods. While vastly inferior in size to the Temple of the Sun at Teotihuacán or the Temple of Quetzalcoatl at Cholula, it nonetheless was one of the largest and had a great architectural and dramatic effect. It commanded the city, the main road led to it, and it could be seen in the clear atmosphere miles away. The word "pyramid" has unfortunately persisted; these were not pyramids in the Egyptian sense, gargantuan tombs for dead kings catacombed within; they were lofty truncated structures on top of which were the temples, which had a real majesty. "The temple capped the substructure and was the culmination of a harmonious series of ascending planes, calculated to increase the illusion of height by emphasizing the effects of mechanical perspective." [58] The religious, administrative, and social aspects of life in the city were grouped, as previously explained, about the temple; this architectural pattern was repeated over and over again, throughout the city. The houses tended to be like squares on a chessboard and formed the basic plan of rectangular rooms set about a patio.

Water was kept potable by flowing through ceramic pipes and was distributed through the city to fountains. The small channels were kept open, the larger constantly cleaned; the engineering works and dikes to prevent the overflow of lake waters and the long causeways to provide access from the mainland to the island temple-city, the removable bridges and sluice gates, all were only part of city planning.

Sanitation was far in advance of anything in Europe until

40. *The building of the principal Aztec pyramid temple, the teocalli, in Mexico-Tenochtitlán. Reconstructed from early Spanish reports, illustrations.*

the end of the eighteenth century. So as not to pollute the lake, excreta was collected and brought to the mainland fields in canoes, to be used as fertilizer; urine was preserved as a mordant for dyeing cloth. Public latrines were seen by the conquistadors all along the causeways.

All this comes from history; there is little or no physical evidence of it. On the mainland, at Tenayuca, six miles north of Mexico, there are remains of an Aztec temple. It was mentioned during the Conquest; battles in 1520 swirled about it. The usually informative Bernal Díaz gives no more than its name, calling it the "town of the serpents." Tenayuca was not originally Aztec, having been built between A.D. 1064 and 1116. On excavating, Mexican archaeologists have found that it was enlarged six times in its history; the last phase, naturally, was Aztec and bears that stamp. Still their architects did nothing to disturb the chain of serpents which flow open-fanged around three of its sides.[58] What there was of its civic center has completely disappeared.

Tepotzitlán, a village fourteen miles northeast of Cuernavaca, has a small temple which crowns the hill overlooking it. A compact edifice once decorated with sculptured façade, it was not in a city, and no other structures remain except this form of truimphant temple erected by Ahuitzotl in 1487, which he dedicated when it came formally within the domains

41. *The ground plans of an architectural complex at Calixtla-*
huaca, close to the circular temple, known as the house of calmecac. *The uneven rectangle measures between* 125 *feet in*
length by 86 *feet in width. Redrawn by Pablo Carrera from a*
drawing by J. A. Gomez, published by Ignacio Marquina in
Arquitectura Prehispánica.

WHAT MEXICO WROUGHT

of the Aztecs. The temple of Teopanzolco, which also lies on the margin of Cuernavaca, is something like Tenayuca, with its exterior and interior stairway. But there is nothing beyond this. No houses stand here. All that is here is a mute symbol of the power of a militant religion. The essential quality of man, the civic city, the living structure of the house, is missing.

Calixtlahuaca, located near Toluca in the state of Mexico, and within the traditional boundaries of Aztec dominion, is an Aztec structure only by courtesy; it was captured by them in 1476 under the reign of Axayacatl and then destroyed by them in 1502. It is so ancient that it has seemingly no precise beginnings; its pottery reveals that the principal temple was begun about A.D. 500.[58] The highest placed site in Mexico, 9,517 feet in altitude, and located near a large lagoon in a valley now entirely devoid of trees, it is famous for its Temple of Quetzalcoatl, which was circular, like the convolutions of a seashell, with doors leading into sealed labyrinths within; outside the traditional stairway mounted. The temple was built and rebuilt as tribes invaded the land and with each new conquest left their impress. In all probability it was one of the first such round structures raised in Mexico. Of particular interest are the remains of the *calmecac* portion of the site; these are the dwellings in which it is presumed the priests of the religious school attached to it lived. These remains give a basic plan of house structure and emphasize what Dr. Vaillant suggested: the most complex Aztec structure is only an elaboration, a large-scale projection, of domestic architecture.

Malinalco, also in the present state of Mexico, is the only site indubitably Aztec that lies outside of the immediate vicinity of Mexico-Tenochtitlán. The monuments and architecture, which date from 1476, during the reign of Axayacatl, were built sixty miles from the city, close to the village of Tenancingo. It is the only temple-city that is partly hewn out of the living rock. It is not, to be sure, a Petra, "the rosered city half as old as time" carved out by the Sîk in Transjordania, nor is it as gigantic as the Egyptian rock tombs of Abu Simbel, but for America it is unusual enough to border on the unique. Malinalco (from *malinalli,* "grass") is self-contained, an architecturally composite site of six larger structures and a number of smaller ones. The principal building is hewn round out of the rock ledge, guarded by squatting pumas. At its entrance is a flight of fourteen steps cut out of the living rock. These lead to a temple, whose door once

42. Plan of the circular temple of Calixtlahuaca. Located within the traditional Aztec territory (near Toluca, state of Mexico), it is 9,517 feet above sea level, close upon the hill named Tenismo. The temple is circular 1), and is approached by pyramid steps 2), in front of which are altars 3). It was surrounded by a wall 4), and other structures 5) served for the ceremonies held there. Excavation shows that it was enlarged many times. Calixtlahuaca has not been definitely placed in spatial culture sequence, but since archaic (B.C.), Teotihuacán (A.D. 500), Toltec (A.D. 1000), and Aztec pottery have been found there, it is presumed that its cultural history covers two thousand years. Redrawn by Pablo Carrera from the original plans of Dr. J. García Payón, published by Ignacio Marquina in Arquitectura Prehispánica.

was the open mouth of a fanged snake head. This gives
access to a circular chamber where eagles with furled wings

43. *Malinalco. A drawing from a wooden drum* (tlapan hue-
huetl), *showing the spirited dance of the Jaguar and the Eagle.
This suggests its dedication to the warrior knights of the Eagle
and the Jaguar. Redrawn by Pablo Carrera from a drawing by
J. L. Quiroz, published by Ignacio Marquina in* Arquitectura
Prehispánica.

and puma heads are carved in the natural rock wall. In another temple there are the remains of an impressive fresco
of marching warriors, typically Aztec, with shields and spears
"at ready." It is believed by Dr. García Payón, who carried
on most of the excavations,[33] that Malinalco was reserved
for the rituals of the military orders of the Eagle and the
Jaguar, the two elite corps of warriors. A beautifully carved
wooden drum found at this same Malinalco confirms this
theory; around it circles a lively dance of jaguars and marching eagles, the symbols of the war cult.

That ends the melancholy parade of what is known of
Aztec ruins, places which even in Bernal Díaz's time were
razed into nothingness, for he wrote: "Of all these wonders
that I then beheld, today all is overthrown and lost, nothing
is left standing."

It shows also how utterly incorrect is the term "Aztec
Empire." Theirs was not, like the Incas' or as the Mayas',
a homogeneous empire, tribe and state; they had dom-

ination—not dominion—over the conquered lands. Held only by troops, there was no political or architectural unity. For instance, the number of Inca structures along the two-thousand-mile stretch of their empire is incalculable, there are so many. And the number of temple-cities in the old and new Maya empire reach beyond a hundred; each year sees more and more sites revealed out of the jungle. Unlike these, the Aztecs had no political method of absorbing the conquered populations into their system and imposing upon them an architectural formula. Theirs was essentially a tribute state. For this reason, to grasp something of Aztec architecture, which had its center in Anáhuac and which was destroyed by the Spanish Conquest, we must turn to those from whom the Aztecs borrowed and adapted.

Teotihuacán, the temple-city of the Toltecs, dwarfs in magnitude all else in Mexico and Middle America. It was in ruins and nameless when the Aztecs knew it. Its Temple to the Sun, 216 feet high and covering ten acres of ground, has no peer; all subsequent pyramids, including the great *teocalli* in Mexico-Tenochtitlán, were stylistically based on it. The remains of this great ceremonial city and center, which alone covers an area of eight square miles (and Mexican archaeologists are the first to admit that they have only found a fraction of the whole), date back to as far as 200 B.C. It continued up to 900 A.D. In this vast extent of time the immense Temple of the Sun, and its heavenly companion, the Temple of the Moon, rose to dominate the long avenues of religious structures which are part of Teotihuacán.

The Toltecs, famed as architects, craftsmen, knew how to handle mass; their buildings are impressive. The decoration, especially in the well-known Temple of Quetzalcoatl, with its great feathered heads as the dominant motif, has a massive awesomeness. Murals uncovered in the temple of agriculture show all the cultivated plants being grown—meaning that every domesticated plant had been developed one thousand years before the Aztecs appeared; the 260-day calendar, great monthly markets, writing, even the familiar Aztec speech scroll—the human tongue wagging in front of the speaker— had already been perfected long before A.D. 500. All were well-worn cultural elements, taken in the whole or inherited by the Aztecs.[81]

Temple-cities are not, to be sure, a purely American phenomenon, as V. Gordon Childe explains in his analysis of similar political systems in the Near East; temple-cities functioned in the same way on the Tigris-Euphrates delta, in the Nile Valley, and in the Indus basin around 3000 B.C. They were the logical outcome of an advance in techniques of agriculture and, with the harvesting of surplus and improved methods of food conservation, the transformation of luxuries into necessities. Since this type of civilization depended on currying the favor of the gods, the result was the temple-city.

As early as 3000 B.C. in Sumer, the temple-city became the repository of social surplus, and that surplus produced a new class of people that never existed when society was in the hunting and fishing stage or at the beginning of agriculture —in short, the nonfarmers, the specialists—artisans, writers, priests.[16]

Tula, which was such a temple-city sixty miles north of Mexico-Tenochtitlán, is also of Toltec origin and very impressive even in its ruins. It is a mutation of Teotihuacán. Until it was excavated by Mexican archaeologists, its exact place in history could not be gauged; now it is fully obvious that it was the model for the Maya site of Chichén Itzá, eight hundred miles distant in Yucatán. Tula originated new design concepts and new god concepts. The central temple is of greatest interest since the two open-jawed, fifteen-foot-high serpents which served as caryatids for the temple are the model for a similar structure in Yucatán; the frieze of marching jaguars and high-stepping eagles is repeated in Chichén Itzá (the same motif was used by the Aztecs in Malinalco); the carved square pillars of warriors are repeated in the Temple of the Warriors in Yucatán; and the vacant stare of the expressionless and terrible figure of Chac-Mool, a prone stone figure which holds a depository for freshly torn human hearts, is also repeated by the Aztecs and the Mayas. All these features had their origin in Tula.

Quetzalcoatl, the culture hero of this whole land, is closely associated with Tula. He was born on what was to be the most momentous date in Mexico, Ce-Acatl, the year of 1-Reed. There was a religious war during his reign, something like the Thirty Years' War in Europe. The city was destroyed, and Quetzalcoatl migrated to Cholula on his way to the coast to his "old home in Tlapálan." The glory that was Tula ended with his departure. Civil war worsened with a succession of "kings" and it was finally destroyed about A.D. 1156, and so it disappeared except in tantalizing myth until the Mexican archaeologist Dr. Jiménez Moreno in 1941 began to clean off the detritus of centuries.[58]

Cholula, the city-state of the Mixtec and now the city of
Puebla, was the next culture to feel the presence of Quetzalcoatl. Forced to leave Tula, he made his way with a good-
sized Toltec force into Cholula; there he stayed and became
renowned as a builder of ball courts and the great pyramid
which bore his name, so large that the people called it *Tlachi-
hual-tepetl,* "Man-made Mountain." This pyramid, torn down
by the Spanish to provide building material for Puebla's

44. *The temple atop the pyramid of legendary Tula or Tollan
(*A.D.* 900–1156), sixty miles north of Mexico City in the modern state of Hidalgo. Tula, belonging to the second phase of the
Toltec empire, was a temple-city, and this, a reconstruction of
what the main building may have looked like, was set on top
of the truncated pyramid. Redrawn by Pablo Carrera from the
water color of Ignacio Marquina in* Arquitectura Prehispánica.

many churches, was measured by Alexander von Humboldt himself in 1804. He found it to be 187 feet high, its base covering the better part of forty-four acres, and it was judged to have been a larger mass than the Egyptian pyramid of Cheops. Its truncated apex, which he sketched, was almost an acre in size; a temple on top of it was dedicated to the god of the Air, which was none other than Quetzalcoatl. The Mixtecs, very advanced in architectural planning and in the making of pottery and in glyph writing, existed as a tribal entity from A.D. 668 until they were overrun by the Aztecs in 1467; their territory spread across the width of Mexico down to the Pacific. When the Spanish arrived there in 1519 they were already under the domination of the Aztecs: "Moctezuma," said Bernal Díaz, "kept many garrisons of warriors stationed in all the provinces"; he had Aztec warriors within and without their capital, Cholula. "The city of Cholula," says Cortés, "is situated on a plain with about twenty thousand houses within its walls and as many in the suburbs outside. . . . The city is very fertile (there is not a palm's breadth of land which is not tilled). . . . There is an abundance of land. . . . As for its city . . . its exterior is as fine as any in Spain . . . I . . . counted more than four hundred pyramids." Bernal Díaz reports in the same vein: ". . . it is a land fruitful in maize . . . full of Magueys from which they make their wine. They make very good pottery . . . and with it supply Mexico and all the neighbouring provinces . . . there were many high towers in the city where the Idols stood, especially the Great Cue [Temple of Quetzalcoatl] which was higher than that of Mexico. . . ."

Although the Aztecs were doubtless influenced by Mixtec-Cholula architectural planning, we have been left no details; like the rest they disappeared totally with the Conquest. While at Cholula, the Toltecs, who were by now reduced to a sort of *condottieri*, made contact with some of the chieftains of Mayapán at the famous trading center of Xicalango, at the edge of Maya territory. There was a civil war in progress in the northern part of Yucatán near Chichén Itzá. The Toltecs entered "in A.D. 1194," says the great Maya authority Dr. Morley, and loaded the scales for victory and gained ascendancy over the Mayas. At the temple-city of Chichén Itzá, at least, they imposed architectural forms that they brought out of Tula. Whether it was Quetzalcoatl as man that led this Maya invasion, or one bearing this name as a patronymic, his name was imposed again on yet another temple-

45. *Plan of the walled ceremonial center of Cempoala, in Vera Cruz, built by the Totonacs and occupied by them when the Spaniards began their conquest in 1519.*

This is the ceremonial center, but the temple-city had a known population of thirty thousand living in its environs. The great plaza had an area of 251,160 square yards. The principal temple 1) was seen and commented on by Bernal Díaz del Castillo. The great plaza 2) was walled, which was an unusual architectural feature. The Temple of the Chimneys 3), a rectangular building attached to the main temple, was occupied by the priests and chieftains; 4) a small edifice called the "Altar" and 5) the great pyramid, explored in the years 1946–47.

city. Myth or fact, Quetzalcoatl was to have a fatal effect on the Aztecs.[81]

The Aztecs, as they conquered, sought new ideas in living and new forms of luxury. They found both in the hotlands of the Gulf Coast. Ahuitzotl during the years of 1486–1503 pushed his conquests to northern Vera Cruz, where he encountered the Huastecs, who were of Maya speech. There he engulfed one of the oldest cultures, which began about 500 B.C.; he found them very well advanced in town planning.

The temple-city of Tamuin, close to the river of the same name in the modern state of Tamaulipas, is especially notable, since its main plaza covered some twenty acres and its temple walls were found to be covered with brilliant frescoes in a style reminiscent of the Toltecs. The Totonacs were the neighbors of the Huastecs. They occupied central Vera Cruz and held dominion over coastal territory close to the Mayas. They were, like the others, occupied by the Aztecs and tributary to them; they also influenced them in architecture. Moreover, many of their temple-cities are still extant, despite the encroaching jungle.

One of these, *Cempoala*, is utterly unique. We have a good description of how it appeared to the Spanish in 1519 to compare with the structure as it has grown out of its present-day restoration.

In 1519 the Spanish were following the ancient coastal road on the way to Cempoala; they passed, says Cortés, "a few large towns very passably laid out. . . . The houses in those parts which can obtain stone are of rough masonry and mortar, the rooms being low and small, very much after the Moorish fashion. . . . Where no stone can be got they build their houses of baked bricks, covering them over with plaster and a rough kind of thatch. . . . Certain houses belonging to chiefs are quite airy and have a considerable number of rooms . . . we have seen as many as five inner corridors or patios in a single house and its rooms very well laid out around them. Each one of the chief men has in front of the entrance to his house a large patio and some as many as two, three, four, sometimes raised a considerable way off the ground with steps leading up to them and very well built. In addition they have their mosques, temples . . . all of fair size."

Cempoala was twenty miles north of the modern port of Vera Cruz. As they approached it and saw the whitewashed buildings rise out of the green jungle, barbarically colored and vibrant, "we were struck with admiration," said Bernal

Díaz. "It looked like a garden with luxuriant vegetation, and the streets were so full of men and women who had come to see us. . . . Our scouts . . . reached a great plaza with courts . . . and it seemed to be whitewashed and burnished . . . one of the scouts thought that this white surface which shone so brightly must be silver . . ."

The whole Totonac land, Cortés estimated, "included as many as fifty thousand warriors, fifty villages and strongholds." The Indians were "of middle height, disfigure their faces in various ways, some piercing the ears, introducing large and extremely ugly ornaments . . . others the lower part of nose and upper lip. . . . They wear as clothes a highly coloured poncho, the men wear breech clouts . . . and body cloaks finely worked and painted. . . . The common women wear highly coloured robes reaching from the waist to the feet . . . but the women of high rank wear bodices of fine cotton, very loose fitting, cut and embroidered after the fashion of our bishops and abbots."

Archaeology has confirmed all that Cortés and his minions said of Cempoala.[58] The temple-city alone with its surrounding houses had a population estimated at about thirty thousand; the walled plaza—which has been measured and in some parts restored by Mexican archaeologists—had an over-all measurement of 210,000 square meters, or nearly 689,000 square feet. The general aspect revealed by research was that it was stone laid with soaring temples. There were fifteen, large and small, within the plaza, the ceremonial center surrounded by one-storied houses, gaily painted and grass-thatched. Dr. J. García Payón, who directed the excavations, found eight large groups of such buildings.

An Aztec garrison was close by. The *pochteca* merchants made frequent visits and the tribute collectors paid semi-annual calls for tribute. Five of them were there at the time of Cortés's arrival, and they were "full of assurance and arrogance," writes Bernal Díaz. "Their cloaks and loin-cloths were richly embroidered, and their shining hair was gathered up as though tied on their heads . . ." The Aztecs thus had access to all this type of town planning and doubtlessly used it. It has been determined that Cempoala was built at the same time as the Aztec sites of Malinalco and Tepotzitlán.

North of this city there are remains of other Totonac city centers. *Tajín,* to name but one, 125 miles in a direct line from Vera Cruz and lying seventeen miles inland, is a temple-city known since 1785. It has been famous since then for its pyramid of the niches. There are 364 niches representing each day of the long year, which is an unusual architectural feature that somehow has withstood the insults of man and time. Mexican archaeologists have found an immense temple-city surrounding this pyramid, with at least fifteen large structures and numerous smaller ones. Here are all the elements of the city: pyramid, ball court, raised terraces, palaces. The ball courts are decorated with bas-reliefs, the style of the figures suggesting Mixtec. The subject matter includes all the familiar motifs used later by the Aztecs; the date 13-Rabbit has been found on one of the stone uprights of the Temple of the Columns. One of the favorite sculptural designs used on the buildings is the *xicalcoliuhqui* "decoration-for-gourds," the most characteristic of Mexican art motifs, derived from the stylized head of the sky serpent, a symbol of Quetzalcoatl.

In the southern highlands of Mexico there are other cultural centers which influenced Aztec architecture. The one that has been the longest known and yet is still the least known is *Xochicalco,* "Place of Flowers" which lies twenty miles south of Cuernavaca. It squats lonely on the highest hills, overlooking two fresh-water lakes two miles distant, in a strongly fortified position. The hills were artificially flattened and terraced, with strong points for defense. Four roads radiate in the four cardinal directions and march up through the impressive buildings into the principal plaza, where the famous Temple of Quetzalcoatl stands. Another temple is reached by a paved ceremonial road sixty feet broad.

46. *Plan of the ruins of Tzintzuntzán. Redrawn by Pablo Carrera from J. A. Gomez, published by Ignacio Marquina in* Arquitectura Prehispánica.

Xochicalco—its true name is unknown—was a ceremonial and, in addition, perhaps an administrative center; all the familiar edifices are here: palaces, temples, the ball court, and, when finally excavated, there will be found a house complex within the temple-city—the famous temple to the Plumed Serpent, which has one of the finest façades in all Mexico, has been uncovered. The handling of the figures would suggest Maya were it not for the fire snakes, which are a symbol of the Mixtecs; the glyphs and dates seem Mixtec and other features suggest Toltec.

Tzintzuntzán, located in the present state of Michoacán, represents a relative rarity. Known in detail only since 1941, Mexican archaeologists found these ruins near the modern village of San Pablo. The ruins, much destroyed by both time and man, have been reconstructed on what is now known. The platform, called *yacata* and approached by the familiar step pyramid, had on its top a concourse of other pyramidal towers. No spatial cycles have yet been put upon it, but Tzintzuntzán is early. Its pottery—an index of time —points to a time between A.D. 500–800.

Monte Albán lies southeast of this city in Oaxaca, isolated from the Mexican plateau by a range of mountains sufficiently difficult to prevent an Aztec invasion until 1469. A composite of cultures, Olmec, Maya, Zapotec, Mixtec, and Aztec, it was perhaps one of the longest continuously inhabited temple-cities known to us (500 B.C.–A.D. 1469). Located on top of the bald hills, 1,500 feet above the level of the valley, although 5,000 feet above the sea, the site has been modified numerous times. When the great Mexican archaeologist Dr. Alfonso Caso first began to excavate it in 1930 and finally concluded the basic part of his work, he found it to be a temple-city set on a large rectangular plaza 2,300 by 820 feet and containing ten large structures: an observatory, a ball court, palaces, and, in the center, a temple complex with four sets of stairways.

There were five marked periods of occupation: Olmec art adorns the early buildings and this links it to the coastal cultures. There followed a period of Maya influence until the Zapotecs exerted their control; this lasted the longest, from A.D. 534 until A.D. 1125. The fourth period found it under the sway of the Mixtecs, who brought new art, new gods, a variation in the calendar, tombs, murals, urns; it was they who made the superbly beautiful goldwork discovered by Dr. Caso in one of the unopened tombs.[11]

Aldous Huxley, when he visited it, found the site "incomparably magnificent. . . . An astonishing situation. . . .

Zapotec architects were not embarrassed by the artistic responsibilities it imposed on them. They levelled the hill-top; laid out two huge rectangular courts . . . Few architects have had such a sense of austerely dramatic grandeur . . . few have been given so free a hand, religious considerations were never allowed to interfere with the realization of a grand architectural scheme; at Monte Albán they allowed nothing to get in the way of the architects."

The fifth phase of Monte Albán was its last; Moctezuma I, surnamed "the Wrathy," set out to conquer Oaxaca in 1469. The Aztecs needed it in order to give their merchants passage down to the Isthmus of Tehuantepec, from there to reach the untouched markets on the western Pacific side of Guatemala and into Central America. They won the temple-city, lost it, and finally, under the next to last leader of the Aztecs, captured it and held it until the arrival of the Spanish. It was well known to the Aztecs and there is definite evidence that they were influenced by its urban planning.

Mitla, called in the Zapotec language *Yoo-paa,* "Place of the Dead," is part of the same culture; it lies twenty-five miles directly south of Monte Albán and is not only one of the best-known sites in Mexico but also the best preserved. There are five groups of buildings, extending to both sides of the mostly dry Mitla River. All of them were constructed with the same basic plan which, Dr. Vaillant has emphasized, characterizes all Mexican structures: rooms formed around a rectangular patio. A cross section of one of the buildings at Mitla suggests how similar Aztec structures were roofed with giant wooden beams. The architectural façade is unique here, although used by the Mayas in Yucatán; the handling of its lines and proportions is unusual. The structures do not stand on pyramids; they are low horizontal masses and have a fortuitous beauty of proportion. There is an austere grandeur in their massive outlines. Aldous Huxley found them "strangely unlike any of the other pre-Colombian ruins . . . the walls of the temples . . . are decorated with geometric patterns . . . all are manifestly inspired by and based upon textile designs. . . . petrified weaving . . ."

All of these temple-cities, and there are many more, were the source of Aztec architectural ideas and Aztec urban planning. It is cause for regret that so much is gone. Yet, if the history of Aztec architecture is so fragmentary it is because there was so little. There was not, architecturally, any such thing as an "Aztec Empire."

27. Sculpture

SCULPTURE was the greatest Aztec contribution to art. A work of art must be measured by its impact, and if one looks at the powerful and awesome goddess Coatlicue, her head of twin serpents, her necklace of human hands and hearts, her arms claw-handed, and her skirt a mass of writhing serpents, it has the same terrible impact that the Assyrian bas-reliefs had on one explorer: "My hair alternately. stood up and flattened down upon seeing them. . . ."

Much of Aztec sculpture is fearsomely awesome; death was much about them and somehow all this feeling that characterized their sculpture had been hammered into the raw stone. It was this that made Élie Faure, the French art historian, blanch and turn aside when he saw it: ". . . beautiful, almost always monstrous, contorted, blown up, crushed in, warped . . . one distinguishes nothing but heaps of crushed and palpitating flesh, quivering masses of entrails, a confused pile of viscera."

Realism was the high quality of Aztec sculpture. There were such pieces as that which revolted our Frenchman, but there are others of much delicacy—a rabbit made of white quartz, limpid and pure and very beautiful, a mask formed out of black obsidian, a woman grinding corn, bending over; sculpture had a wide range made to be seen from all sides. It was not like the Maya work, which Aldous Huxley described as "profoundly, incommensurably alien." Aztec sculpture had an uncanny vitality and unself-consciousness that makes it appeal to the modern eye. As the very observant Pál Kelemen wrote: "The nature of sculpture and the inherent possibilities in the material . . . make it perhaps the most immediately comprehensible of all the arts." [47]

Aztec idols were fearful things to the Spanish; they felt their impact. Thus José de Acosta: "They call this idoll *Tezcallipuca*, he was made of a blacke shining stone [obsidian] like to *iayel*. . . . It had earrings of gold and silver and through the nether lippe a small cannon of crystal. . . ." Yet an Aztec sculptor could handle material ranging from an emerald the size of a pea to immense masses as large as the great calendar stone, weighing twenty-four tons. His tools were the simplest: stone celts, awls, and drills.

Sculpture was closely linked with architecture. Almost in every structure extant one sees how closely allied were these two functional things—there were sculptured friezes, enormous stone-carved caryatids, columns; sculpture was not a superficial element as in our concept, but a fundamental part of architecture. All of their art was purposeful, functional, and it belonged to religion. *L'art pour l'art* had no meaning in Aztec life. Art was purposeful and hieratic; religion was life and life was religion, and sculpture along with all their crafts was tied to it. This is equally true of almost all the art forms of the other tribute states, Babylonia, Assyria, and Egypt.

Aztec sculpture subordinated detail to them—they had none of that fear of empty space which caused the Mayas to overcrowd design with detail; their aim was impact. The stone piece of Xipé has the flayed god appearing so simply quaint it seems as if the sculptor's small child was the model, until, looking at the back, one becomes aware that Xipé is attired in a freshly flayed skin of a sacrificial victim.

Different from all these and buried in a mass of ritualistic detail is the Aztec calendar stone. Two years in the carving (1479–81), it stood twelve feet high and weighed twenty-four tons. It embodies "a finite statement of the infinity of the Aztec universe," with the face of the sun god Tonatiuh in the center and twenty names of days circling it; it is filled with symbols of previous world epochs, symbols of heaven and color—a grandiose conception of the universe.

Aztec sculpture has quality. One does not have to be versed in all the intricacies of religious symbolism to enjoy it. Pál Kelemen wrote that it could be enjoyed as pure sculpture detached from any precise culture.

28. The Lapidaries, Goldsmiths, and Jewel Carvers

METALWORK came late to Mexico. It came up by slow degrees from South America.

None of the early cultures worked metal; it does not appear at Teotihuacán, which was already a memory when the technique of gold and copper working reached Mexico. It was unknown to the early Mayas, and the Olmec craftsman contented himself with making diadems of jade. It was not practiced in Mexico much before the eleventh century.

Gold makes life sumptuous; the Aztecs knew it and traded for it. As Bernal Díaz saw it, it was free to be traded in the market places: "placed in thin quills of geese, so that the gold could be seen through it."

Mining was rudimentary. Gold was panned or collected in nuggets; silver, which seldom occurs pure in nature, was more of a problem and was less used. Gold is a metal of great ductility, for a single grain can be drawn into a wire five hundred feet long. It was worked by the Aztecs with the simplest of techniques. It was melted in a furnace heated by charcoal, draft being supplied by a man blowing through a tube into the charcoal embers. There are few implements extant but we have been left illustrations of goldsmithery. They worked the gold by means of hammering, embossing, plating, gilding, sheathing. Out of this simple, almost crude technique came gold pieces which excited more than the cupidity of the conquistador. There were "three blow guns," said Bernal Díaz, "with their pellet molds and their coverings of jewels and pearls, and pictures of little birds covered with pearl shell."

Most of the gold extracted from Moctezuma, some 600,000 pesos weight of it, was melted down into ingots; some of it they thought too beautiful to destroy, like the pieces they received

at Vera Cruz at the beginning of the adventure: "a wheel like
a sun, as big as a cartwheel, with many sorts of pictures on it,
the whole of fine gold; and a wonderful thing to behold . . .
Then another wheel was presented of greater size made of
silver of great brilliancy in imitation of the moon . . . Then
were brought twenty golden ducks, beautifully worked and
very natural looking, and some [ornaments] like dogs, and
many articles of gold worked in the shape of tigers and lions
and monkeys . . . Twelve arrows and a bow with its string
. . . all in beautiful hollow work of fine gold." [25] All this
was sent intact to Charles V. He being then in Flanders,
Cortés's ship was sent after him. He was at last found
in Brussels, and, on July 12, 1520, Cortés's ambassadors
presented the Aztec goldwork to him. His comment, whatever it was, has not been recorded. That gold, like all the
rest that came from the Americas, went into his crucibles to
be made into ingots to pay the soldiery to maintain him on
the nebulous throne of the Holy Roman Empire. Fortunately the great Albrecht Dürer was there at the same time and
he left his impressions of it in his diary. Himself a descendant of a line of Hungarian goldsmiths settled in Nuremberg,
knowing what he was seeing, Dürer wrote:

I saw the things which were brought to the King
[Charles V] from the New Golden Land [Mexico]; a
sun entirely of gold, a whole fathom broad; likewise a
moon entirely of silver, just as big; likewise sundry
curiosities from their weapons, arms and missiles . . . all of
which is fairer to see than marvels. . . .
These things were all so precious that they were valued
at 100,000 gulden. But I have never seen in all my days
what so rejoiced my heart as these things. For I saw
among them amazing artistic objects and I marvelled over
the subtle ingenuity of the men in these distant lands.
Indeed I cannot say enough about the things which were
there before me.

That was the only commentary on these things by anyone
whose opinion meant anything. Charles V ordered that
henceforth all gold and silver coming from the Indies be
melted down on arrival. Little survived—except the wonderful descriptions of the conquistadors, which, since there was
no gold later to be found or seen, historians of the eighteenth century took as the natural braggadocio of such men.
It was only in 1931 when Dr. Alfonso Caso found the

undisturbed tomb of a Mexican chieftain at Monte Albán, containing superbly beautiful necklaces, earplugs, and rings, that historians realized that the simple, honest Bernal Díaz was making a magnificent understatement.

Goldsmiths had a guild. Those attached to Moctezuma's many-roomed houschold were nontaxpayers; they were supplied with placer gold and busied themselves making pieces for Moctezuma and other officials. Bernal Díaz speaks of the "workers in gold and silver . . . and of these there were a great number in a town named Atzcapotzalco, a league from Mexico." Since the gold was sold in the market, presumably any craftsman who had enough to barter for the goose quills of gold dust could work it up into jewelry for himself or else for trade.

Lapidaries, workers in precious stones, were many, and like the others: "skilled workmen Moctezuma employed." [25] Foremost of the stones was jade. This was found in southern Mexico and Guatemala and valued more than gold itself, which Bernal Díaz found to his satisfaction, for he took four jades during the first Spanish retreat from Tenochtit-lán and they "served me well in healing my wounds and gathering me food."

Jade was an article of tribute and the glyph for it is found in the Book of Tributes. Now there is a difference, mineralogically, between the jade of America and that of the Orient, which should put to rest the idea that the American Indian got his jade from China; it is "American." It is utterly amazing how the Aztec craftsman achieved the delicate handling of so hard a stone; it required great patience. Everything of jade was saved, even the smallest pieces of the "precious green," to be put in the mouths of the dead to take the place of the stilled heart.

Masks were often made of jade, or, when it was not available, of less valued greenstone. Masks, with their expressionless slit eyes and swollen lips, were a feature among all of these cultures. Some are exquisite, others are repetitious and "vulgar," as the astute Pál Kelemen noted. These powerful artistic impulses "were stereotyped through constant repetition." The truth is that most art has always been either bad or indifferent, as Aldous Huxley said when looking at the same thing: "Vulgarity is always the result of some excess; and the means to vulgarity are therefore means to the realization in practice of an inward tendency toward the excessive." This holds for any who dominated: "Vulgarity has always been the privilege of the prosperous . . ."

The skill among the lapidaries was broad; the large objects doubtlessly were done by the "professionals," yet much was done by the ordinary craftsman. Crystal, a very hard stone, is not easily worked, yet the Aztecs shaped art forms out of it from the smallest of pieces to the life-size crystal skull. This latter symbiosis of beauty and death sits, divorced from its conception, before black velvet curtains in the British Museum.

Turquoise came by trade from the north. It was much in demand and traveled almost as far to Mexico and Yucatán as did amber (that "special act of God") in the Old World. The Aztec exacted turquoise as a form of tribute and it so appears from eleven towns on the tribute rolls; it was used with other materials for the making of mosaics on masks, knives, and even walls.

Obsidian glass was an Aztec specialty; it was exported as raw material and as finished product. Found close by, a product of volcanic action, obsidian was used for knives, razors, lip plugs, mirrors of high polish, and other objects of immense beauty.

Emeralds (*quetzal-itzli*) were the prize gem for the Aztec as for the Spanish. "The Kings of Mexico didde much esteeme theme; some did use to pierce their nostrils and hang them therein," says José de Acosta, "on the vissages of their idolles." As soon as Moctezuma was elected as Chief Speaker, the first thing he did was "to pierce the gristle of his nostrils, hanging thereat a rich emerald."

The conquistador saw them as a symbol of riches. Hernán Cortés commandeered the whole of them for himself; he knew that Cleopatra wore emeralds and that a Christian pilgrim lately from India saw them in a temple of Buddha, "flashing their fire two hundred leagues on a cloudless night." As for the source, Moctezuma expressed ignorance; they were from "the south." In fact, they were from only one region, the mountain areas in Colombia, about Muzo, which was the only source of emeralds at that time. They were plenteous in Colombia, where they were used for barter to obtain cotton and gold dust. They were well known in Panamá and used to great effect in combination with gold. They were obtained for Moctezuma by the activities of his *pochteca* merchants who penetrated beyond Nicaragua. Emeralds are soft and chip easily, yet the Aztecs cut them in intricate patterns—flowers, fish, fanciful forms of exquisite workmanship. Hernán Cortés got his emeralds directly from Moctezuma, one in a pyramidal shape, "broad as the base of the hand," others so fabulous that Charles V is said to have coveted the fantastic baubles. Cortés refused 400,000 ducats in Genoa for them, saving them for Doña Juana de Zúñiga, his betrothed, a daughter of a ducal family. He gave her five Aztec-worked emeralds, "one in the form of a rose, one like a bell with a pearl for a tongue, one like a fish, one like a trumpet, one like a cup." [56]

29. Feather Weaving

THE FEATHER weaving was another of the Aztec accomplishments. Examples of it have disappeared completely because of conquest and climate. The only examples of real magnificence of this art are preserved by mere accident of history. The rest has perished. Similar feather weavings found in the desert coast of Peru, well preserved despite the passage of time, have given us an idea of the technique; we also have illustrations of artisans weaving feathers in the work of Bernardino de Sahagún.

Feathers weavers (*amanteca*) were highly appreciated; they formed a guild and were of the professional class. In feather weaving, quills were inserted into the web, each quill was hooked over a thread and secured by a knot in the second row, leaving only the color part of the feather visible on the other side. The color pattern had to be carefully arranged as a mosaic before the feathers were applied. Shields, headgear, cloaks, banners, totem emblems were all done in feather weaving. Warriors so accoutered die beautifully.

Since colorful birds were limited in the altitudes of Mexico-Tenochtitlán, there was much activity on the part of the merchants to obtain bird feathers when the local supply did not meet the demand.

Birds of all climes were brought alive to Mexico and their habitats simulated; the waterfowl alone had separate pools, as attested by Hernán Cortés: "ten pools of water in which were kept every kind of waterfowl known." There was no such thing in Europe until Padua in 1545 erected a zoological garden. The type of food and water depended on the bird. There were three hundred men employed to look after them and "each pool was overhung by balconies cunningly arranged from which Moctezuma would delight to watch the birds." In another part were cages for the land birds, wooden trellises cleverly made, 9 feet high and 18 feet around; there were another three hundred men to look after these. Bernal

Díaz could not even name all of the various species that he saw in that aviary: "birds of great size, down to tiny birds of many-coloured plumage . . ." The birds bred in the cages, too. As they molted, the feathers were gathered, selected, graded, and brought to the feather weavers.

Let no one doubt the magnificence of this art. One piece has been preserved, the headdress sent by Moctezuma to Hernán Cortés when he first landed at Vera Cruz and was believed to be Quetzalcoatl returning to reclaim his empire. This was sent in turn to Charles V, who passed it on to his fellow Habsburg, Archduke Ferdinand of Tyrol; it was long preserved in the castle at Ambras. When discovered and its history made known, it was sent to Vienna, and there today it rests in a burst of golden-green iridescence in the Museum für Völkerkunde—a double assurance, if that be needed, of the Aztecs' sense of beauty.

Everyone in Aztec society was some sort of craftsman. "Art" as a name for this is in all probability not the right word, yet is there another? The Aztec was a maker of things; everything was functional, real, purposeful. As Aldous Huxley pointed out when he examined all this for the first time: "Craftsmanship brings psychological fulfillment, a society of craftsmen is a society of satisfied individuals." More, it had a human wholeness. "A primitive is forced to be whole—a complete man, trained in all the skills of the community, able to fend for himself in all circumstances; if he is not whole, he perishes." But was the Aztec impressed by his craftsmanship, his "art"? Dr. Vaillant thought not: "They did not speculate about aesthetics." Yet a Mexican sociologist, going through Nahuatl texts,[50] believes they did and that they were animated by a real sense of beauty. He has translated the "song of the painter":

> The good painter,
> understanding god in his heart,
> defines things with his heart,
> dialogues with his own heart.

The Nahuatl texts now made available to us [34] show many expressions that suggest this attitude was not an isolated instance. In the presence of his "art" the craftsman felt the divinity of things. For listen to the song, well remembered and sung over and over again to later generations, of a bird-keeper who saw death fall upon Mexico-Tenochtitlán and the aviaries which he cared for all perish in the flames:

> *the plumes of the quetzal*
> *the works of iridescent jade*
> *all broken and gone*
> *the memory of a beautiful world,*
> *god-filled, truth-filled . . .*

If then, this real feeling is true, how explain the other world of the Aztecs, the "apparent incongruity," as Prescott wrote, "of a comparatively refined people of often gentle influences whose religion was of a spirit of unmitigated ferocity." Why did the Aztecs inhale the perfume of corpses as if it were some aphrodisiac perfume?

30. Religion, War, and Administration

WAR AND RELIGION, at least to the Aztecs, were inseparable. They belonged to each other. "It is no exaggeration to say," observes a recent writer on the subject,[19] "that the government of [Aztec] Mexico was organized from top to bottom so as to be able to sustain, and thereby mollify, the unseen powers with as many human hearts as it was possible to give them."

Blood was the drink of the gods. To obtain appropriate prisoner victims as sacrifice for the gods, there were ceaseless little wars, for one could hardly expect the Aztecs to offer themselves in endless lines for immolation. At the outset it would serve little to explain this attitude in moral terms. All militant religions have been involved in bloodletting in one form or another.

The object of Aztec religion was to attract favorable forces to it and repulse or at least mollify those which were not. They knew that nature moved in a series of rhythmic patterns. They put all their observatory powers to work to discover what these rhythms were and to harness them, not alone for their own good but for all mankind's survival. "From this point of view," wrote Dr. Alfonso Caso, "magic and science are alike: both are techniques which aim at the control of the world and both consider that magic or nature are a necessary link between phenomena." [12]

Since man always turns things into an image of himself, it would have been impossible for the Aztecs to have a mental image that was not anthropomorphic; natural forces among them were personified. As the society grew complex, the gods grew in complexity and they took on specialized functions.

In the forefront of the Aztec pantheon was a sun god who brought life by his daily appearance; sun worship was an essential part of Aztec religion. There were the gods of the four cardinal directions, each symbolized by his own color,

"since," as Dr. Vaillant wrote, "the Aztec universe was conceived on a religious rather than a geographic sense." Gods
were appointed, with their colors, in keeping with the preconceived prejudices of their own life history: east was red;
south was blue, and evil; west was white (it had good auguries); north was black, a pallor of gloom and presided over
by Mictla-tecuhtli, Lord of the Dead.

There were personal gods, each plant had its god, each
function its god or goddess, even suicides had one. Yacatecuhtli was the deity of the merchants. In this polytheistic
world all gods had clearly defined traits and functions. So
the pantheon grew more complex as the people took to wor-
shiping the different manifestations of the gods, and this
duality made the pantheon so bewildering that only the
priests, whose function it was, could keep track of them all.

The Aztec gods warred in Aeschylean grandeur. The gods
of evil—for the Aztecs believed in immanent evil—fought
with the beneficent gods. Light and darkness struggled for
man's soul.

Yet all this was beyond the pale of mere man. He kept to
the little gods. The image of the corn goddess he purchased
at the market—a stamped clay figure which he buried in his
milpa field with prayers and tears. There were household
gods set up in some remote corner. There was the goddess of
the maguey, Mayahuel, whose spirit was evoked when he
drew the sweet syrup and converted it into an intoxicant.

All these earth gods were their life. The complicated religious pattern they left to the priests, who told them when
to weep, when to get drunk, when to rejoice, when to die.
The people seemed content to resign themselves to those
who spoke of the unknowable with so great a certainty.

Huitzilopochtli, the Hummingbird Wizard, was the Aztecs'
own. They were his children, the "chosen people." He it was
who led them out of the dry misery of the north into the
promised land of Mexico-Tenochtitlán; he took his place
among all the other gods, from the ancient past and from
other cultures. He was the sun, the ever-youthful warrior
who fought battles with the other gods for man's survival.
Each day he rose, fought the night, the stars, the moon, and,
armed with sunbolts, brought on the new day. Since he
fought these battles for them, the Aztecs could only repay
him by nourishing him for his eternal wars. The proffered
food could be neither the watered-down intoxicant pulque,
nor corncakes such as mortal man ate—the god must be
nourished on the stuff of life: blood. It was the sacred duty

of every Aztec—for all were part of an agrarian militia—to take prisoners for sacrifice in order to obtain for Huitzilo-pochtli the nectar of the gods—human hearts and blood.

War, eternal war, then, was bound up with religion. How else could human hearts be obtained? A long peace was dangerous, and war thus became the natural condition of the Aztecs, for if the beneficent gods were not nourished they would cease to protect man from the other gods, and this might lead to the total destruction of the world. When the great temple pyramid to Huitzilopochtli was dedicated in Mexico in 1486, "king" Ahuitzotl, after a two years' war campaign in Oaxaca, amassed more than twenty thousand prisoner victims. These were lined up in rows waiting to be spread-eagled over the sacrificial stone. Their hearts were cut out and held briefly to the sun, then, still pulsating, deposited in the heart urn of the recumbent Chac-Mool figure.

The ritual for all this became as complex as that which now surrounds the religion Norman Douglas described as the "quaint Alexandrian tutti-frutti known as Christianity."

The priests directed the intellectual and religious life of Mexico. At the top of the pinnacle was the Chief Speaker—the "king," to the Spanish. He was more than an ex-officio high priest; his was the final tribunal.

Two high priests (*quequetzalcoa*) lived in Mexico. Under them was another who administered the business end of tribute tithes and who supervised the schooling of new priests (*tlamacazqui*) and the establishment of the faith in the newly conquered villages. There were, it is said, five thousand priests attached to the temples in Mexico-Tenoch-titlán alone. They dressed in black, their *tilmantli* were ornamented with a border of skulls and entrails. Bernal Díaz said that the priests had "long robes of black cloth and long hoods like those of the Dominicans . . . The hair of these priests was very long and so matted that it could not be separated or disentangled . . . and [it] was clotted with blood."

They elaborated cult rituals, taught in the religious schools, helped train those who traced out the rituals, worked with the *tlacuilo* artists, taught and extended the knowledge of hieroglyphic writing and the symbols of the complicated mathematical and astronomical computations. They helped the architects to delineate the temples and buildings, and when the buildings were completed arranged the ritual of sacrificial dedication. They helped to create music and dances, arrayed them, prescribed the things to be heard, proscribed those not to be heard. They intervened with the unseen powers, remembered and chanted the historical events until they became fixed in human memory. This theocracy pervaded everything in Aztec life.

"The gods ruled," wrote Dr. Vaillant, "the priests interpreted and interposed and the people obeyed."

31. The Calendar

THE CALENDAR was at the base of every action of the Aztecs.

There were two calendars, the ritualistic one (*tonalpohualli*) * a parade of 260 days; and a second which was a form of solar calendar. The latter consisted of eighteen 20-day months, a lunar reckoning of 360 days plus five uncounted days, the empty *nemontemi*.

The first calendar was magical and sacred; it bore little relation to astronomical observation, and the origin of the cycle has never been satisfactorily explained. It was very ancient; the Aztecs gave it nothing, for it had been known to the Mayas under the name of *tzolkin* for fifteen hundred years. The divinatory cycle consisted of twenty periods of thirteen days. There were twenty day names—*calli* (house), *coatl* (snake), *malinalli* (grass), *tochtli* (rabbit), etc.—which, combined in sequence with the numbers one through thirteen, designated the days, such as 1-Grass, 2-Reed, 3-Ocelot, etc., to 13-Lizard, when the next period began. In this example, the name "Grass," coming up in its regular position, would coincide with the number 8 in this next period, followed by 9-Reed, 10-Ocelot, etc., to 13-Motion. This pattern recurred again and again in a continuous fifty-two-year solar cycle, or 18,980-day period, in such a way that no day could be confused with any other, since the name of the day and its associated number precluded repetition within the fifty-two years. Each year was named after the day on which it began; thus a year known as 1-Reed would recur every fifty-two years.

The solar "year-bundle" (*xiuhmolpilli*), as the Aztecs called it, consisted of 365 days, divided into eighteen months of twenty days each. The remaining five, "the empty days"

* This is often mistakenly called the *tonalamatl*, which is really the physical book in which the *tonalpohualli* was recorded.

Miquiztli   Mazatl·   Tochtli   Atl

Itzcuintli   Ozomatli   Malinalli   Acatl

Ocelotl   Cuauhtli   Cozcaquauhtli   Ollin

Tecpatl   Quiauitl   Xochitl   Cipactli

Ehecatl   Calli   Cuetzpallin   Coatl

47. *Aztec day signs. A solar calendar was divided into eighteen 20-day months (with five empty days); the sacred calendar was divided into twenty 13-day months. The day signs were used in both calendars.*

(*nemontemi*), were the unlucky days and neither named nor counted, just as in New York City many buildings do not have a thirteenth floor.

The least common multiple of 260 (20 by 13) and 365 (whose primes are 5 and 73), as Franz Boas graphically explained,[5] is 18,980 days. This was the fifty-two-year cycle; after this period the same divinatory combination repeated itself. In another form the Aztec astronomer-mathematicians, or those from whom they obtained this most complicated, ingenious calendar, determined that seventy-three years of the divine calendar (20 by 13 by 73) resulted in the same 18,980 days, making again the magical fifty-two-year cycle.

Why this fifty-two-year cycle? Why was fleeting time so great an obsession with the Aztecs? Why did it become a national fetish so that they really believed that at the end of a fifty-two-year cycle the very future of the world was in balance and might be destroyed? Did the very cleverness of the mathematicians seduce them? Did the fact that these two calendars just happened to coalesce in the various calculations to make the fifty-two-year cycle seem so magical that they conceived their inventions to be really a basic fact of nature? No one really knows.

The Aztecs' relation with time was fundamentally emotional. Their priest-astronomers had put great intellectual effort into the elaboration of the calendar. As a calendar, it was more advanced than in either Egypt or Greece. Egypt and Mesopotamia had lunar calendars, i.e., the beginning of every new month was determined by the waxing or waning of the moon. They made up for the discrepancy between lunar and solar by having "hollow" and "full" months, and this crude form of calendar existed down to Roman times. All peoples strongly agricultural in character gave great importance to the solar year, but the cities in the Fertile Crescent had different calculations, which produced chaos in comparative time reckoning. The Egyptians (as did the Mayas and Aztecs) had two systems: a religious lunar calendar and a civil 365-day calendar; and a twenty-five-year cycle.

The Greeks in the time of Hipparchus (150 B.C.), taking over the whole of Babylonian science, began to use "the methods of computing sexagesimally and the place-value notation, including a symbol for zero," [64] but the use of the zero symbol never came into general practice until the Hindus perfected it in the eighth century A.D. Yet the "American" cultures were far, far in advance of all this; the Mayas invented zero and could calculate their day count as far into the past as 23,040,000,000 days.[64]

Why all this? Why this extraordinary preoccupation with time? Did they find the endless continuity of time so appalling even though they marked it into spatialized periods with rituals and festivals? No one knows. The dominant note was the fifty-two-year cycle; the whole of the tribe's intellectual forces was put to work long before its advent to allay the wrath of the gods.

The priests had to calculate ritual by most involved methods; they had to know the precise interconnection between each particular god and "time" as given on the calendar. Sacrifice had to be correctly calculated so that it would benefit the particular god to whom they were appealing. All the developed intellect of the Aztec was turned toward this one thing: how to propitiate the right god at the right time. So sacrifice was not mere butchery, it was a parade of elaborately conceived ritual with only one object in view: to preserve human existence.

For the Aztec was threatened not only at the end of each fifty-two-year cycle; when the priests announced the end of each year there came the dreaded *nemontemi,* the "five empty days." Fires were extinguished, fasting was general, sexual intercourse ceased; artists left off their work, business lay idle. The same thing occurs in the Austrian Tyrol when the *Föhn*— the warm south wind—blows: important business grinds to a halt. No transactions on these days have legality. On the dawn of the fifth day, when the priest-astronomers, consulting their calendar books, observed the Pleiades rising in the heavens and knew the world would not end, they reached out and found a sacrificial victim, slashed open his chest, pulled out his heart, and in the freshly weeping wound kindled a new fire; from it all the fires in the temples were rekindled; and from it people all over Mexico-Tenochititlán gathered the new fire for the new year.

All was right once more with the Aztec world.

32. War and Weapons

WAR was the director of this religion.
It was, as is seen, related directly to religion (captives for sacrifice). It was related to economy (supplying tribute for the tribute state). War was an Aztec preoccupation; it was sacred; it had a mystic religious quality which made it all the more ferocious. Every able-bodied man was a warrior, part of an agrarian militia; the only professional army in the Aztec confederation was the small coterie of well-born warriors who formed the bodyguard of the Chief Speaker. The Aztecs had universal service hundreds of years before Napoleon returned to nature by using a mass army without regard to losses (instead of the artificial maneuvers with small bodies of troops favored in Baroque times). The Aztec warrior was hard and .spartan; he was trained to be so from childhood. His land was not lush, life was not easy, he was given only one choice: victory or death by sacrifice. Life, if it would be great, the Aztec attitude emphasized, is hard, and to victory belongs the sacrifice of victory.

War is the primary of politics. It was to the Aztecs then; it is the same to us, the living. Politics is the way in which a fluid being maintains itself, and the character of war and politics is quite the same: [87] tactics, stratagems, material forces applied at the moment of truth are the same in both, ". . . the growth of one's own way of life at the expense of the other." [75]

War as a branch of politics began with the powwow. Ambassadors, called *quauhaquauh nochtzin,* were sent to the village or tribe under pressure to join the Aztec "commonwealth"; trade and road protection were offered. With the compact came the demand that the Aztec national god Huitzilopochtli be placed alongside their local deity. They were to be allowed to keep their own dress, manners, and chieftains; they would yield tribute every six months.

48. *Aztec warriors, showing their weapons, elaborate headgear (to aid in overawing the enemy), shields, and face painting, all part of war equipment. The round object was a shield (chimalli) which bore the crest of the clan. The most-feared weapon was the* maquahuitl, *the sword toothed with obsidian blades; there was also a sort of tomahawk. The bow (tlauitolli) was a Toltec weapon, used by the Aztecs and introduced into Maya country in the tenth century. The javelin (mitl) was thrown with the aid of a spear thrower and had great force.*

Negotiations were long and involved; [81] they were given the length of a lunar calendar month to capitulate.

When war was decided in council, the leaders gathered in front of the stone of Tizoc in the great plaza. Set up during the reign of Tizoc (1481–86), the large cylindrical block of trachyte, eight feet in diameter and carved with figures in low relief, shows Aztec warriors capturing others in battle, symbolized by the warrior grasping a lock of the enemy's hair. [72] It was set up facing the great *teocalli;* there or near to it the final act of war was set in motion.

The war lord held office only for the duration of a particular campaign. He was generally related by blood ties to the Chief Speaker. His war dress was elaborate; there are murals still extant that show him accoutered in quetzal feathers, ofttimes with a fantastic headgear. It was impossible not to discern him in battle and one of the prime objects was his capture. The elite of battle, the military order of the Eagle, wore a mimicry of an open eagle's beak and feather weavings of eagle feathers; the military order of the Jaguar dressed in jaguar skins; the soldiers, other common warriors from the clans, wore distinct tunics. Their shields also bore a totemic device of their clan. Before they set off, priests had to consult the *tonalamatl* to divine if the moment was propitious for victory. And why not? The Incas consulted the lungs of sacrificed llamas to see if the auguries were right, the Romans consulted chicken livers; the Aztecs, consulting the stars in their orbit, were at least a bit more governed by reason. If observations suggested dubious victory, they did not enter into war until later.

The Aztecs, in comparison with the European standards of 1519, were lightly armed. Headgear when worn was more decorative than protective. They did, however, wear quilted cotton tunics, soaked in brine; as Bernal Díaz observed, they "wore armour made of cotton reaching to the knees." For the hot country it was superior to Spanish armor. All carried shields (*chimalli*) to deflect arrow or sword. Made of wood covered with animal hide, many were extremely decorative, with the totemic device of the clan. The closing-in weapon was the *maquahuitl;* it was of hardwood edged with blades of obsidian sharp enough for a warrior to sever a horse's head. The bow (*tlauitolli*), with obsidian-tipped arrows, they used with deadly effectiveness "and with great skill," confesses Bernal Díaz, who received many in his own hide in his time; "the first flight of arrows wounded fifteen soldiers." In addition to these they had the sling,

which hurled an egg-sized stone, and, most effective, the
obsidian-tipped javelin (*mitl*), which was thrown with great
force by means of the *atl-atl* spear thrower. Bernal Díaz remembered that in one of their battles on the coast, the Indians "let fly such a cloud of javelins . . . that they wounded
seventy of us."

The nature of the land conditioned Aztec strategy. Wars
had to be of short duration. They had no beasts of burden;
everything had to be carried on the backs of human carriers.
There was no system of supply such as the Incas in Peru set
up along finely developed roads. Siege wars under these conditions were almost impossible since no Aztec army could
be kept on the field for more than a few days. Besides, the
Aztec plan was not to slaughter unnecessarily or destroy;
death and destruction would imperil tribute, which was the
primary aim of the battle, along with the need for sacrificial victims.

In general there were no walled cities, although the Mayas
had several in Yucatán and the hereditary enemies of the
Aztecs, the Tlascalans, built a wall fifteen feet high surrounding their large towns.*

The watery defense of Mexico-Tenochtitlán was a deter-
rent to any save the Spanish but in general there were no
fortifications. Fighting was in the open. There were no "se-
cret weapons," all had the same type of arms; what counted
most in battle was surprise, ambush, morale. Battle began
with a war of nerves: there were military promenades to
overawe the enemy; warriors came with drums, conch-shell
horns (the type seen in the Maya murals at Bonampak). The
Spaniards in their first encounter got the same treatment; the
Indians were "drawn up in battle array whistling and sound-
ing their trumpets and drums." [21]

Before the campaign got under way, ambassadors had to
be sent to towns and villages, subject or not, to arrange for
supplies. It was almost impossible to hide intent in a major
undertaking. In some instances the Aztecs deliberately re-
frained from use of surprise, not only giving their enemy
time to arm, but sometimes even sending them arms, to develop the premise that the outcome on the battlefield was, in
truth, the will of the gods.

When at a distance of an arrow flight from each other, the
opposing warriors released their shafts over the heads of their

* A part of this defense wall can still be seen at Huexotla
(state of Mexico).

forward forces; then they hurled rocks, accurately enough, from plaited cotton slings. Spears followed, which really wrought havoc, then in a welter of noise and fearful shouting they fell on each other with the *maquahuitl,* the closing-in weapon. The object was to capture the leader. Often this alone was enough to decide the issue—a single battle could suffice; again enmities could be protracted over the years. Slaughter was only to cause a rout; when that happened prisoners were taken. The retreat was followed up by the Aztecs into the principal tribal city; usually the priests with some warriors put up a determined resistance on the steps of their sacred *teocalli.* In token of victory the Aztecs burned the temple, for that was the symbol of conquest in their glyph writing. Peace was arranged as quickly as possible and normality restored. Then the tribute tribunal fixed the amount and kind to be yielded every six months. The warrior-prisoners were sent to Tenochtitlán to be held for sacrifice; if the tribe was unreliable, an Aztec garrison was placed close by and their chieftains were sent as hostages to the Aztec capital. No attempt was made at absorption of the newly conquered into Tenochtitlán. "The idea of absorbing conquered towns into the victorious state . . . never occurred to the Mexican," says Dr. George Vaillant, "and even defeated towns retained their local autonomy." There were revolts, naturally, and the Aztec militia had to be kept constantly on the go; this one defect in their political system was their Achilles' heel.

There never was an "Aztec Empire." They were never able somehow to transform domination into dominion.

33. The Tribute State

THE AZTEC state was a tribute state.

Although trade was vast, extending down to Nicaragua and perhaps beyond, although things Mexican traveled as far north as Arizona for an interchange of products (Moctezuma was said to have had a bison in his zoological gardens), although the Aztec people were good craftsmen and produced for "export"—still the state in its later development depended on tribute exacted from conquest. The Aztecs knew, without the benefit of an Oswald Spengler, that "war is the creator and hunger the destroyer of all great things" and that whole peoples have lost force through the gnawing wretchedness of living. When an Aztec warrior died, he died *for* something, not *of* something. Total war was not part of their policy, nor did they want to liquidate or force the erstwhile enemy into abject poverty; they wanted tribute.

This imperial appetite began after A.D. 1400. It continued under the various "kings" until by 1519 the Aztecs dominated—with tribute yield—those parts of Mexico beginning in the north about Tampico across to Lake Chapala, thence southward including almost all of the southern part of Mexico up to the domain of the Mayas. It was large enough to include 371 tribute towns and sufficiently complex that they had to keep tribute rolls so extended that Hernán Cortés had to admit to his King-Emperor: "I was unable to find out exactly the extent of Moctezuma's kingdom. . . . The king has fortresses in all those provinces armed with his own men and also overseers and tax-collectors." And: "the tribute is inscribed in written characters and pictures." These were the tribute rolls (or, since they were folded screenwise—

books), the same that Bernal Díaz saw at Tenochtitlán: "a great Cacique . . . kept the accounts of all the revenue that was brought to Moctezuma, in his books which were made of paper which they call *amatl*, and he had a great house full of these books."

A copy of one of these is still extant, with names, products, and amounts from tribute towns. Antonio de Mendoza, the first viceroy to Mexico (1535–49), had one of these tribute charts copied. It was drawn by a native artist, the glyphs translated and written in parallel Spanish orthography. It was intended as a gift to Charles V; instead French pirates seized the Spain-bound vessel at Vera Cruz, and by a chain of events too complicated to follow, it came to rest in

49. *The collecting of tribute was done every six months. Various objects of tribute collected from conquered tribes or those living under Aztec hegemony are seen here. There is a shield, blankets,* huipilli; *in another section Indians bring in corn and squash. One of the tribute collectors studies the tribute charts.*

the hands of André Thévet, the famous cosmographer to the King of France. He sold it for twenty crowns in 1584 to the English traveler and publisher of discoveries, Richard Hakluyt; it was translated with the idea that Sir Walter Raleigh would publish it at his expense, but he left his head at Whitehall before this could be accomplished. It then came into the hands of Samuel Purchas, the clerical publisher of travel literature, and so it first appeared in *Purchas his Pilgrimes* in 1625. After being "lost" for two centuries in the Bodleian Library at Oxford, the *Codex Mendoza* (named after the one who had had it made), was included, in 1831, in Lord Kingsborough's *Antiquities of Mexico.*

Tribute covered every phase of Aztec wants and Aztec luxuries. Foremost were various elaborate war costumes: helmets, shields, jaguar skins for warriors of that order, eagle skins of the other; other clothing included all that man wore in Mexico.

Precious stones formed an important part of the tribute list: gold, turquoise, and jades are listed; gourds, copal for incense, copper, shells, skins and bird feathers, dyestuffs, cotton, rubber—all were part of the economy. Chocolate, which every well-placed chieftain quaffed, flavored with honey, vanilla, and, of all things, red pepper, must have come to Tenochtitlán in great quantities: "it seems to me," wrote Bernal Díaz, "that they brought out . . . over two thousand jugs of cacao all frothed up . . ." Foodstuffs were a dominant item in the tribute rolls; one can see very clearly the quantities of corn, beans, pepper, honey, vanilla that made their way into the Aztec capital.

The *calpixque,* tribute collectors, were naturally hated and feared. Their arrival every six months to supervise collections meant that towns had to disgorge much of their surplus. A good description of the *calpixque* is in the literature; they appeared in 1519 at the selfsame Totonac villages in Vera Cruz then occupied by Hernán Cortés and his small army: "five Mexicans, who were Moctezuma's tax-gatherers, had just arrived. . . . [They approached] with the utmost assurance and arrogance . . . Their cloaks and loin-cloths were richly embroidered, and their shining hair was gathered up as though tied on their heads; and each one was smelling the roses that he carried, and each had a crooked staff in his hand. Their Indian servants carried fly-whisks . . ." [25]

The Vera Cruz area was garrisoned by Aztec warriors; some were at Ceycoccnacán, said Hernán Cortés, "a fortified town which belongs to Moctezuma," so that any discourtesy to the tribute collectors or any delay could bring swift retribution.

To give historical balance, not all tribes nor all towns under Aztec dominance were in opposition; the Aztec overlords freed them from the petty tribal struggles, commerce widened, prosperity was heightened by protection, roads were freed from attack, and Tenochtitlán was a good consumer. Many accepted the Aztec peace willingly.

Who had title to the tribute and how did it enter their

economy? Presumably the state, i.e., the Chief Speaker, who officially received the tribute at his capital. There, as we know, it was entered into his "account books." Some of it, such as excess foodstuffs, must have been distributed to the various clans on arrival; some of it was stored in the official storage chambers to be used against periodic famine or to pay, in lieu of money, the wages of those specialists attached to the royal household. Bernal Díaz said that "Moctezuma has two houses full of every sort of arms . . . There were shields great and small, and a sort of broad swords . . . lances . . . which cut like razors . . . quilted cotton armour . . . casques or helmets made of wood and bone"—all the things that appeared on the tribute-lists.

Distribution of all this was made on a per capita basis. Aztec society existed for the good of the whole people, and while the tribute won by Aztec armies was in practice held by the Chief Speaker, all of it, in one way or another, found its way back to the people. Arms were distributed to each clan and held in part of the local temple; foodstuffs were distributed. Doubtless, based on the designs of the shields, each clan had the right to ask a tributary village to make shields carrying their own coat of arms on it. Some of the tribute was used to pay the tax-free artisans, the specialists —priests, masons, goldsmiths, featherworkers, sculptors, etc. —who produced the vast array of beauty which the public enjoyed.

Such a tribute state is not new in history; as has been pointed out, it has its parallel in Sumer, which, around 3000 B.C., maintained itself similarly. Before 2500 B.C. all the temple-cities of Mesopotamia within the same general region had been independent states until Sargon of Agade extended his conquests "to the silver mountain and the cedar forest," making, like the Aztec, a conquest of all the petty states and forcing tribute from them in the form of raw materials, and this imperialism "became a new instrument in the concentration of a still vaster social surplus." [16]

It was not enough that the Aztec state was a tribute state, for while the common man did not own land, he owned— after work tax—the usufruct of the worked lands. Surplus was traded at the various markets; leisure time used up the raw materials which filtered down from top to bottom and were made into manufactured goods for "export" trade. So, to extend this economy, a new class came into being—something unknown among nations of other indigenous "American" organizations—a merchant class.

34. *Pochteca:* The Merchant Prince

THE GUILDS of "commercial travelers," the *pochteca*, were a law unto themselves. They had distinct prerogatives. They lived in their own wards or *calpulli* (Pochtlán was one); guild rights passed from father to son; they paid no taxes; they had their own gods, and before setting off on a long journey they evoked the protection of Zacazontli, the protector of roads and travelers; and they were not subject to the ordinary law tribunals.

The *pochteca* were a rather late development in Aztec society. Their own chronicles said, "commerce began in Mexico-Tenochtitlán in the year 1504"; assuredly it was earlier. It rose out of the great social surplus piled up in the city as a result first of tribute and then of the manufacturing activities of a people somewhat relieved from constant attention to agriculture. In and about the city they manufactured cotton cloth, rabbit-fur robes, obsidian and copper mirrors, cosmetics (a tincture of cochineal with grease) for face painting, medicinal herbs, flower pastes as a base for perfumes. Salt, which they leached out of the lakes, and other stuff that was light enough for long journeys, were also in the list. In return for these things the directing classes and the common man alike wanted from the hotlands cotton, feathers, precious stones, chocolate, rubber. The *pochteca* were purveyors of luxuries.

All of the early Old World routes were luxury routes: the amber road (still known as the *Birnsteinstrasse* where it passes through Bamberg, Germany) was the longest haul in ancient times—from the Baltic to Egypt. From 10,000 B.C. people journeyed these thousands of miles to obtain amber.

Salt, a luxury for many, made one of the great life lines in history. The *Via Salaria* was one of the first Roman roads. Grain eaters needed salt; for them it was an essential. Those in highland Mexico who had no coastal connections were dependent on the Aztecs who controlled the salt-leaching works about the saline lakes. One of the plaints of the chieftains of the Tlascalans, hereditary enemies of the Aztecs, was that "they had no salt; since there was none on their lands and they did not venture out." [21]

Still the greatest traffic has always been in luxuries. It was frankincense and myrrh, or silk loaded on camel caravans, or delicacies for "frolicking and chewing and sucking" for Greek or Roman banquets. In the New World the Aztecs craved chocolate and feathers, jade, emeralds, and gold dust. The *pochteca* in this world were the alchemists who turned the base metal of necessities into the gold of luxuries.

Trade was a monopoly of the *pochteca*. Days, weeks, months were spent by them acquiring the articles for trade at the various markets; they then assembled carriers who were capable of carrying sixty pounds on their backs, and the human caravan set off. In regions where conditions were not fully secure they were accompanied by Aztec warriors. Trade has always been sacrosanct. The way to bring down swift reprisal was to plunder them. If one of their numbers died in a far-off land he was given the same rites as a warrior slain in battle.

50. *The* pochteca *were commercial travelers of the imperial Aztecs. With the aid of their human carriers, they extended Aztec commerce as far south as Nicaragua.*

Aztec trading colonies under the *pochteca* penetrated to Guatemala, going down the Pacific Coast (which was not controlled by the Mayas) as far south as Nicaragua. Their caravans were often gone for a full two years. They also left colonists behind, small "islands" of Nahuatl-speaking peoples called *pipil*, who, even now, show their Nahuatl origin in their designs on pottery and weaving and their use of the symbol of Tlaloc, the Aztec rain god.[55]

The *pochteca* were often accused of being "warriors in disguise," [81] ferreting out information as to the weakness and strength of tribes outside the pale of Aztec dominance. There seems to be no direct evidence of this, but as conquest often followed their trading incursions, the "other peoples" received them suspiciously when they bore gifts.

35. Roads, Transport, Couriers

Little is known of Aztec roads or communications. That there *were* roads and good communications must be assumed. Yet there have been no connected studies of Aztec roads such as have been made of the network of the Maya *sacbeob*, nor has there been such an extensive survey as the von Hagen expedition study of the Inca highways on the west coast of Peru.[87]

The best-known Aztec road, since it was the one that Cortés and his small army followed from the hotlands to the uplands of Mexico, was that which ran from Vera Cruz to Mexico-Tenochtitlán; the precise route has been identified. The first prerequisite of empire is communications. Rome had it, the Incas had it, but since the Aztecs were not an empire, their roads were undeveloped. The nature of Mexican geography worked, it is true, against direct communications, and the engineering science of the Aztecs was not oriented in the manner of Peru. Yet the Incas would have found Mexico's obstacles minor; they had roads that crossed the bare Andes as high as 15,000 feet.

Roads in Mexico followed the path of least resistance. The ancient trade route was on the warm Gulf Coast, the main road which ran from Xicalango (Sahagún called it "the land of Anáhuac Xicalango") as far north as the Tropic of Cancer. Xicalango was located in the Laguna de Términos, into which four rivers debouch. Here Maya trading missions had contact with central Mexican tribes. It is from here that Toltec troops were introduced into Yucatán in the twelfth century; it was from Xicalango that the Aztecs had first news of the arrival of white man.* It was one of the great trading centers of central Mexico; trade from Yucatán

---

* Sahagún said: "They had news of the arrival of the Christians from some merchants [*pochteca*] who had gone to the markets of these coasts . . . at Xilanco [Xicalango]. . . ."

and Central America was brought to it by giant canoes arriving along the coast.

The road ran northwest from here along the jungle coast through the Olmec country into the lands of the Totonacs where a road (followed by Hernán Cortés and his small army) led to their villages, and to the large city of Cempoala. Cortés does not describe it. There were no bridges—rivers which rose with callous ease would not permit them, and natives crossed by canoes or by swimming. In fact, in all Mexican literature there are no descriptions of bridges other than the small removable ones used by the Aztecs in their causeways. Presumably this coastal road continued up as far as Tampico (22° N. lat.).

Mexico-Tenochtitlán was connected with a road from Vera Cruz and the conquistadors followed it. Only from them do we have a description: "The way was rugged"—understandably, since it rose from sea level to 8,000 feet; in a few miles it was narrow. When they entered Xicochimilco (now Xico) in the heights, it was defended by "a town of great strength" and the road "was a narrow defile cut in steps." Beyond this the road passed through the frigid unpopulated heights of Cofre de Perote (13,000 feet), where the traveler was assailed by "whirlwinds of hailstones and rain."

Once the land mass lowered into a warmer plateau, Cortés speaks of a "royal road"—it is not further described. They found rest houses at intervals and occasionally small temples "with idols" which Cortés likened to roadside chapels built along Spanish roads. Near to Cholula they found two roads: "The best road was by way of Cholula," now the city of Puebla. This "royal road" passed between the volcanoes of Popocatépetl and Ixtaccihuatl ("my men proceeded along it until they came to two mountains between which it runs"), and went straight to Mexico-Tenochtitlán by way of the town of Amecameca; another branched off to Chalco near to the lake's edge and it was "well swept and clear."

Along this route, which is often subject to sleet and snow in the winter, there were way stations like the Inca *tampus:* "groups of houses which they build like inns or hostels where the Indian traders lodge." At the edge of the lake they entered the wide causeways which lead to the capital of the Aztecs.

Some of the Aztec roads were doubtlessly paved with *tezontli,* a pink pumice traprock, abundant and easily worked, composed of silica and volcanic ash. This is suggested by the fact that the name of the god of the road

whom all travelers invoked was Zacazontli. But there is little physical evidence of pre-Hispanic paved roads throughout Mexico. There are remains of ceremonial ways at Teotihuacán; there is a sixty-foot-broad paved road at Xochicalco
that leads to a hilltop temple, but it is only half a mile in
length. There is nothing like the Maya *sacbeob* ("artificial
roads") built of limestone with a width of 15 feet, rising
above the plain and extending for 62.3 miles from Cobá to
Yaxuna in Yucatán.[82]

Two roads went southwest out of Mexico-Tenochtitlán.
One was that already described which ran through the snow-
topped volcanoes to Cholula and on southward to Oaxaca
toward the Pacific; the other leaving Mexico went due west
of Cuernavaca and paralleled the first to Oaxaca, making
junction at Huajolotitlán; it then proceeded to the Pacific
Ocean, terminating at Huatulco. There seems not to have
been any direct Aztec communication to the Pacific Coast;
indeed, there was no need for it. The Aztecs did not use the
sea; they had no maritime connection with any other land,
and there is no evidence of any direct communication, to
use an example, between Mexico and Peru. All the evidence
has been sifted; there were no communications between the
Inca Empire (or those that preceded it) and the cultures of
Mexico. The Spaniard had to develop Mexico-Peru communications *ab ovo*.

The southern communications of the Aztecs—a mere development from existing older routes—we know only because after his Mexican conquest Hernán Cortés used the
road, enlarged it, and created a port at the Indian fishing
village of Huatulco on the Pacific (the best natural port
southward from Acapulco). The manner in which Cortés
enlarged the ancient trails to provide space for cart traffic
suggests how it was done under the Aztecs. The work of
building and maintaining the roads, writes Dr. Woodrow
Borah, who was the first to thread his way through the maze
to plot the road, was carried out by *corvée* levied on Indian
towns near by. Each village took care of the twenty-mile section nearest it. They also maintained the inns or *mesones*
on the route. The southbound Aztec-Zapotec road joined up
with another transcontinental route at Tehuantepec, which
crossed the flat isthmus at sea level. Where precisely the
southbound road went from there is conjectural.

Although the Aztec reached considerable heights in luxury, he never escaped carrying his own burdens. The llama
and its relatives were unknown in Mexico until the estate of

51. *Water transport was limited to lakes. The canoes were as large as the trees which could be brought down. Although the Aztecs had some coastal trade, this was usually carried on by allied tribes.*

Hernán Cortés (Marquisate del Valle) brought a herd of sixty llamas, *"ovejas del Perú."* [1] They were taken to the highlands of Penol del Xico for domestication in Mexico; they died out and that was all. Although most Indians carried their own produce, there were some of the baser sort who formed the human caravans. These *tamenes* were well-known; Bernal Díaz called them *hombres de carga:* "There arrived thirty cargo-Indians called *tamenes*. . . ." The regular accepted weight was a little less than sixty pounds, the rate of travel fifteen miles a day.

The wheel, except as used in children's toys, was totally absent in Mexico. The whole principle of the wheel as arch was unknown, as was the potter's wheel and the rotary quern. Even if the wheel had been known, it is doubtful that it could have served much without draft animals. Instead the Aztecs used the litter. This conveyance for the exalted was universal in the Old World as well as the New; few advanced cultures were without it. The Aztecs seem to have considered it only a ceremonial device and not, as among the Incas and the Chimús in South America, a mode of transport. To the Spanish, Moctezuma first appeared being carried in a litter along the great causeways out of the city. There is no mention, however, of the litter being used beyond this; when Cortés took along the unfortunate last Aztec "king," Cuauhtemoc, on his expedition to Honduras, he walked as did the rest of the Indians.

Water transport was limited to the lakes. The Aztecs constructed dugout canoes—almost everyone seems to have had one in this Venice-like city. Much of the lacustrine commerce was carried on by water. Canoes brought in produce. They removed the excreta from the public toilets so as not to pollute the city and used it for fertilizer. There were special canoes used to transport fresh water: "The water is sold from canoes," wrote Hernán Cortés. "The canoes place themselves under the bridges where the aqueducts are to be found

52. *Courier runners employed to carry messages over Aztec roads.*

. . . filled by men who are specially paid for this work." The Aztecs used no other type of boat larger than the dugout; when Cortés built two moderate-sized sloops on the lakes of Mexico, he took the captive Moctezuma for a sail to a distant isle, skimming over the wind-swept waters, so that "Moctezuma was charmed and said it was a great thing, this combining sails and oars together." [25] The Aztecs had nothing larger than these for the Pacific; in the Gulf the Mayas had enormous dugouts, and Caribs sailed the turbulent seas with no difficulty, but the Aztecs like the Incas were landlubbers.

Couriers were employed on the roads to carry messages. Beyond the fact that they existed there is little more reference to them, whereas those Spaniards who went from Mexico to Peru were astounded at the Inca system of *chasquis*, who, running in relays, could cover a distance of 1,250 miles in five days. The Aztec courier was trained to run; there were competitions for the fleet of foot and this tradition is still kept up by the present-day Tarahumara Indians living in Chihuahua.

Pictographic communications were put into a forked stick. It is not known for certain but it is probable that an artist accompanied the runners on important missions. At Vera Cruz Cortés was amazed upon receiving an embassy from Moctezuma who "brought with them some clever painters . . . and ordered them to make pictures true to nature of the face and body of Cortés and all his captains, and of the soldiers, ships, sails and horses . . . even of the two greyhounds; and the cannon and cannon balls . . ." [25] Later he found when in Mexico that Moctezuma had known by such means every action of theirs since they touched the shores of Mexico.

Thus the Aztecs had roads, wayside rest houses, roadside gods, couriers, and, through their pictographic writing, a good form of communications. The Europe of 1519 had not as much. "To journey in Europe," wrote Awaliyal Effendi in 1611, ". . . is like a fragment of hell." Roads in the sixteenth century were paved like hell in the proverb, and many the complaint that travel was a purgatory "in little." To move over Europe's roads one had to have "a falcon's eye, an ass's ears, a monkey's face, a merchant's words, a camel's back, a hog's mouth, a deer's feet."

It is small wonder that the conquistadors praised the Aztec roads.

36. Paper, Writing, Literature

A LL ADVANCED civilizations (with the amazing ex-
ception of South American cultures such as the
Inca, Chimú, Mochica, and Tiahuanaco) had some form of
paper, some form of writing, and some form of literature.
In all these phases of culture the Aztecs excelled.

Paper (*amatl*) was an article of tribute.

On the tribute lists of Moctezuma one reads: "twenty-four
thousand reams of paper are to be brought as a tribute
yearly to Tenochtitlán." Twenty-four thousand of these
reams would be 480,000 sheets of paper and judged by any
standard this is an enormous consumption of paper.* [18]

While it is not necessarily true, as someone once wrote,
that the quantity of paper consumed stands in direct ratio
to the intellectual development of a people, still the prevalence of paper and writing had much to do with the particular intellectual direction of the Aztecs.

"True paper" (the product of a technique by which beaten
fibrous material is felted on a mold while suspended in water)
was not the paper of the Aztecs. The inventors of true paper
were the Chinese in A.D. 105. They used the fibers of the mulberry. The technique was transmitted by Chinese papermakers captured by the Arabs in 751 after the battle of
Samarkand. Papermaking was perfected by the Arabs,
brought by them to Spain in 1150 when they settled in Xativa,
from whence paper went around the Western world. [42] The
Egyptians did not have true paper either; papyrus was made
by laminating strips of the stems of a water plant; they were
able to produce rolls of papyrus "paper" twelve inches wide,
forty feet long. The most widely used method of obtaining
a paper substitute, the one used by peoples in such widely

---

* "Ream" is adapted from the Spanish *resma,* which in turn is
derived from the Arabic *rizmah,* "a bundle, especially of paper."
It is only an expression which fortuitously coincided with the
Aztec numeral *pilli* and has no connection with our ream.

53. *Two forms of Aztec papermaking. On the left, an Indian pulls off the bark of the wild* Ficus *tree (related to the mulberry which is also used in papermaking). The bark was then beaten into large rolls of paper which were folded double to make books. On the right, a woman makes smaller pieces of paper from branch fibers of the same tree.*

separated regions as Polynesia, Melanesia, Southern Asia, Africa, South America, and the method that was the source of Maya and Aztec paper was that of peeling off the bark of the *Ficus*, which is related to the mulberry, and felting it into sheets as thin as paper by beating it with a ribbed mallet. This is called "bark cloth," but it is not cloth since it is not woven; it is bark paper.

A functional form of paper made in this manner appeared very early in Yucatán and Mexico. There is no manner of dating its appearance, but probably it was used as paper among the Mayas as early as 1000 B.C.[84] The Mayas folded their *huun* paper and made polychromic books of it. The paper prepared from the inner bast fibers of the wild fig trees was, in use and appearance, like true paper. There are only three such Maya "books" or codices left of those that escaped the "burning of the books" in Yucatán by Bishop Diego de Landa.

All of the advanced cultures in Mexico had paper and writing. The Toltecs had glyph writing and the same graphic techniques; they are credited with having an encyclopedic *teoamextli,* a divine book compiled in A.D. 660; neither it nor others like it have survived. The Mixtecs at Cholula had paper and writing; several of their codices are extant. So did the Zapotecs in Oaxaca and the Totonacs in Vera Cruz. Bernal Díaz saw piles of books near the Totonac city-state of Cempoala: "Then we came on some towns . . . [and] found idol houses . . . and many paper books doubled together in folds like Spanish cloth . . ."

Paper and writing, then, were not an Aztec invention; the Aztecs, however, perfected them.

The fact that the Indians had books and writing greatly astonished the conquistador: "There is so much to think over," said Bernal Díaz, "that I do not know how to describe it, seeing things as we did that had never been heard or seen before or even dreamed about." So much so that they sent back to Spain, along with the first gold collected, two of such books. Fortunately these fell into the hands of the Italian humanist Pietro Martire d'Anghiera, who was then in Seville; he, corresponding with the learned, wrote about "books such as the Indians use." Later Dr. Francisco Hernández, who was neither priest nor clerk, came to Mexico in 1570 in the capacity of *protomédico* on the first botanical expedition to the new world. In the course of his five-year plant explorations he saw the paper craft at Tepotzitlán: "Many Indians are employed at this craft. . . . The sheets of paper are then polished (by means of a *xicaltetl*) and fashioned into sheets." These *xicaltetl* were stone flatiron-shaped celts which, when heated and pressed upon the paper, closed the pores and gave it surface, more or less the same technique that European papermakers used during the Renaissance to burnish paper by means of an agate stone. "It is something like our own paper," he wrote, "except that theirs is whiter and thicker." The paper was called *amatl,* the tree the *amaquahuitl* (literally "paper tree"), of the genus *Ficus.*

The Aztec glyph for *amatl* was a roll. Yet there were other types. A yellow paper always sold in sheets came from the town of Amacoztitlán on the Rio Amacuzac in the state of Morelos; it derived from the fibers of the yellow wild fig, the *Ficus petiolaris.* This whole area, in a tropical setting of under 5,000 feet, was *the* paper manufacturing center of ancient Mexico. Itzamatitlán, a village in Morelos on the Rio Yuatepec, was the source of yet another type of paper.

The Aztecs were like the Chinese in their reverence for paper, for "all classes of Chinese," writes Dard Hunter,

54. *Three types of Aztec* amatl *paper:* 1) *A paper roll attached to the symbol for 8,000.* 2) *A yellow paper, made in sheets, which came from the town of Amacoztitlán. Above the paper are teeth symbols for* tlan *(place); below, the symbol for water.* 3) *A long roll-type paper (which came from the town of Itzamatitlán) made from the* Ficus *tree, whose leaf was shaped like a dagger* (itzli).

"from the aristocratic scholar . . . down to the most illiterate coolie [showed] a pronounced reverence for every scrap of paper." This, more or less, was the attitude of the Aztecs.

Paper on arrival went first to the priests, writers, artists; then it passed into the market where it was purchased or traded. Bernal Díaz saw it there: "[There was] paper, which in this country is called *amatl* . . ." Sahagún, the observant Franciscan monk, in his great work on the Aztecs (in the chapter entitled "The Gods Which the Ancient Mexicans Adored") tells us that "for the merchant's god Yacatecuhtli . . . they made offerings of paper . . . for the image of Napatecli—the patron god of the rush-mat makers—they gave him a crown of paper . . . and in his hands flowers made of paper." Each of the Aztec months dedicated to a god was "honoured by strips of paper covered with copal and rubber . . . for the goddess who lived in the house of the sun . . . they adorned with paper." So it went on, every phase of life or worship used *amatl* paper. Even today the descendants of the Otomis remain papermakers. They make their paper from the same plants as did the Aztecs.

The greater bulk of the paper, however, was used to keep the genealogies, trial records, land records, for each ward or *calpulli* had its land registers and tribute rolls. There were hundreds, perhaps thousands, of such "books." Bernal Díaz thumbed through them when he wandered into the endless rooms of Moctezuma's palace; he followed an "accountant" and he saw "all the revenue that was brought . . . [and recorded] in his books which were made of paper which they call *amatl*, and he had a great house full of these books."

Those not destroyed by the Spanish siege of Mexico perished in other ways. After the Conquest Fray Juan de Zumarraga collected all the "books" that could be found, especially in the "royal library" at Texcoco, east of Mexico, and "the most cultivated capital of Anáhuac," wrote Prescott, "and the great repository of the national archives." The "burning of the books" by the monks was so thoroughly done that only a pitiful fourteen of these now remain.

Like all early writing, Aztec writing was nonphonetic. It was not capable of any general statement nor could abstract ideas be expressed. Only in its later evolution was a change sensed and the Aztecs seemed to be arriving at the beginning of syllabic phonetics. This would have occurred when signs no longer stood for pictures, or even ideas, but for sounds. Instead, Aztec writing, in 1519, was still pictographic: a wrapped mummy figure was a symbol of death; migrations

55. *An illustration showing the comparative glyph writing of
the Egyptians and the Aztecs.* ABOVE: *A detail from King Narmer's palette, Hierakonpolis, Egypt, 3100* B.C. *The first sign of
the man symbolizes a fish, the n'r fish and its phonetic value*
nar. *The second sign represents a chisel,* mer; *hence the name
of the king, Narmer. Narmer holds a warrior by the hair—the
symbol of captivity. Above this a falcon sits on six lotus buds.
Each lotus* (kha) *has the sound value of a thousand. So it is
read: "King Narmer brings six thousand foreigners captured
within their land."* BELOW: *An arrangement of Aztec history,
as given in the* Codex Mendoza, *to show similar thought and
glyphic pattern. This depicts one of the military achievements
of Moctezuma I (1440–69). A rebus drawing of his name is
above. An Aztec grabs the hair of another—the symbol of battle.*

or movements along the road were expressed by footprints; seeing was expressed by an eye projected beyond the viewer; speaking was a wagging tongue; a mountain was symbolized so obviously that even one untrained in reading Aztec glyphs would know it. These symbols could be compounded so that if a "rememberer" wished to chant about a notable historical fact such as *"In the year 2–Reed (1570) Moctezuma conquered the village of Itztepec,"* the *tlacuilo* artist would have first drawn the year 2-Reed, then the official accepted symbol of Moctezuma; a thin line would have run to a burning temple and above it the rebus drawing of the town of Itztepec (an obsidian dagger on top of a mountain).

There was naturally no alphabet to this system, yet the Aztecs did combine a series of pictorial elements, often abstract, to give complicated meanings; by these methods as well as by puns, color, position, they produced a staggering amount of records.

The thought of God and the exigencies of economy were the origins of writing; at least this was true in the Near East. Early Sumerian writing (about 5000 B.C.) developed as did the Aztec. The clay tablets were impressed, says Dr. H. S. Hooke in *A History of Technology*, with a cow's head, an ear of grain, a fish, a mound; later they were compounded and show the "first attempts to express verbal notions." By 4000 B.C. the Sumerians had a syllabary or sign-list of five hundred to six hundred signs. Egyptian writing developed similarly. The motive that furthered writing was the need to record tribute. In the temple-cities of the Near East, God was regarded as the owner of the land and the people as occupiers of the land, and they had to pay rent to the temple-city, to the priests who were the gods' vicars.

In the beginning early Egyptian pictorial writing did not differ a great deal from that of the Aztecs. Later, in the Middle Kingdom, it was reduced to 732 conventional signs, moved into syllabary, developed homonyms, and, as it progressed, divorced sound from meaning. Still later it evolved into a cursive form of glyphic script and by 800 B.C. into demotic, which is one of the forms found on the Rosetta stone. In the beginning the pictographic glyph to express a historical event was not much different. Take for example a

To the right is a symbol of a temple on fire, meaning conquest; attached to the temple is the rebus drawing of the village, a tree which has a speaking tongue—Quanahuaca (modern Cuernavaca). Above it is the date, 1469.

historical event of King Narmer's dated 3100 B.C.[39] This is a mixture of pictorial and phonetic elements: *"King Narmer brings six thousand foreigners captured within their land."* When the two forms of writing are compared in descriptions of similar events, they tend to show similar evolution.

This speaks very well for the perception of the Aztec, for although his cultural attainments appeared forty-five hundred years later in time than those of the Egyptian, it must be remembered that man migrated to the Americas during the early Neolithic stage of his history. At the time of the early American's arrival into the Americas the other Neolithic cultures, in the Middle East, Europe, Greece, had no greater wit nor ornament than he. But the "American" became isolated from the main currents of cultural evolution. The art of writing, the wheel, the alphabet, metalworking, etc., came out of the Fertile Crescent and thence made their way throughout the Old World. Even then diffusion worked slowly. It took two thousand years for the principle of the wheel to reach Britain and other inventions were even longer in arriving.

"The fabric of the Old World history," writes Pál Kelemen, "is like a vast web stretching from the Roman ramparts of England to the delicately drawn woodcuts of Japan, from the Byzantine icons of the Russian steppes to the wondrous world of the royal tombs of Egypt. . . . It is an enormous territory . . . yet remote as certain points lie from one another, as different the styles, it is clear that details and even whole ideas were incorporated, adapted, and developed interregionally."

The Aztecs had literature. The term perhaps is incorrect, just as saying that their functional crafts were "art" is not wholly right; while both expressions are true, they are, in fact, misleading. As is obvious, the Aztecs had no literature as we understand it, even though the word can be defined as "the total of preserved writings belonging to a given language or people." Yet, since one must always put a truth or a conclusion at the end of a chain of reasoning, like the knot at the end of a thread—since otherwise the thread would not hold—so therefore Aztec literature.

Aztec literature was mostly history. Annals of ancient times, year counts, books of the day and the hours—even diaries. There were observations of planetary events, eclipses, movements of stars, observations of celestial phenomena which had affected or might affect their present. There was much out of the past; for their mythopoetic faculty was well developed. They were poets and most delighted when writing and singing of the past—for only the past, is really poetic. One of their chief concerns was this; their "histories," recorded on paper, showed the migrations, the stopping-off places, the wars, conflicts, founding of cities. Their sacred almanacs were scarcely literature nor were their tribal records, land registers, lines of descent, and tribute charts.

Their tribal history approached more closely to what we know as literature. Even then, what was put down was only enough to aid the memory; there were no cross references to other tribes. The Aztecs would have seemed to any who read their glyphic charts as if they lived alone in Mexico. No reference is made to other tribes. Aztec interests extended "vertically from tribe to pantheon." [81]

Aztec literature really consisted of that which was unwritten, that which was transmitted orally, and glyph writing served to provoke the memory of the "rememberers," helped them to recall the passing of events. These twice-told sagas, hymns, elegies, chants only became "literature" when they were set down by a bilingual scribe (Spanish Nahuatl) after the Conquest.[34]

Many of the great sagas which form our world literature were orally transmitted before they were set down. For how long were the wanderings of Ulysses chanted before some nimble-fingered scrivener put it down? All the stories of the Cicones, the Lotophagi, the Cyclops, and the Laestrygones were repeated in chant before being made "immortal" by letters.

And so with Aztec literature. Present-day Mexican scholars, who speak Nahuatl as easily as they do mellifluous Spanish, have translated the original texts set down by scribes who transcribed them from the original sixteenth-century Nahuatl speech. Dr. Angel María Garibay has filled two volumes of things Aztec (which are here translated into English for the first time), and it is amazing how wide the field of the Aztec concern was. Reading them we are brought in closer connection with these people whose spectacular history has here been set down. They were always curious about their relation to the universe as a whole; they questioned themselves about life and afterlife.

> Is it true that one lives only on earth?
> Not forever on earth: only a short while here.
> Even jade will crack,
> Even gold will break,

> *Even quetzal feathers will rend,*
> *Not forever on earth: only a short while here.*

Those who may go into the place of the underworld chant about the day:

> *[If] in one day we leave,*
> *In one night descend to the mysterious regions,*
> *Here we only came to meet,*
> *We are only passers-by on earth.*
> *Let us pass life in peace and pleasure; come, let us rejoice.*
> *But not those who live in wrath: the earth is very wide!*
> *That one could live forever, that one need not die.*

The poetic side of their lives, their imagery and the love of nature and flowers, which even Hernán Cortés first recognized, is expressed in an agony of soul:

> *My heart wishes with longing for flowers,*
> *I suffer with the song, and only rehearse songs on earth,*
> *I, Cuacuauhtzin:*
> *I want flowers that will endure in my hands . . . !*
> *Where shall I gather beautiful flowers, beautiful songs?*
> *Never does spring produce them here:*
> *I alone, torment myself, I, Cuacuauhtzin.*
> *Can you rejoice perchance, may our friends have pleasure?*
> *Where shall I gather beautiful flowers, beautiful songs?*

The *Codex Florentino*, written in Spanish, translated directly from ideographic Nahuatl speech, sermoned how the boys studying in the *calmecac* religious schools "must learn artfully all the songs, the songs of the gods . . . which are written in the books," such as these:

> *Where shall I go?*
> *Where shall I go?*
> *The road of the gods of duality,*
> *Could your house perchance be the place of the fleshless?*
> *Perchance inside heaven?*
> *Or is only earth here,*
> *The place of the fleshless?*

And others, which reaffirmed God's possession of this celestial globe:

> *In heaven you live;*
> *The mountains you uphold,*
> *Anáhuac is in your hand,*

> *Everywhere, always you are awaited,*
> *You are invoked, you are entreated,*
> *Your glory, your fame are sought.*
> *In heaven you live:*
> *Anáhuac is in your hand.*

One American scholar, John Cornyn, opines that in the whole range of indigenous "American" literature no other tribe has left such a variety of expressions and feelings. For it is through chants that literature left the realm of the priestly intellectual and entered the people. Here they stress ideas, both hieratic and secular, a fact unusual in itself. A poet, perhaps a worker in fine stones, sings of the beauty of gems:

> *Jades I perforate, gold I cast in the crucible:*
> *This is my song!*
> *I set emeralds ...*
> *This is my song.*

And that he *felt* as a literate artist feels is expressed by the phrase "understanding God in his heart":

> *The good painter;*
> *Toltec artist of the black and red ink*
> *Creator of things with the black water. . . .*
>
> *The good painter; understanding*
> *God in his heart,*
> *Defines things with his heart,*
> *Dialogues with his own heart.*
>
> *He knows colors, applies and shadows them.*
> *Draws the feet, the faces,*
> *Sketches the shadows, obtains a finish,*
> *As if he were a Toltec artist*
> *He paints the total colors of flowers.*

Does one suspect these sentiments? Does it appear that the original Nahuatl-Mexican text has been improved in the translation, gilded by Spanish poets who love to tint the past with new colors? This is how a fragment of the original text appears in parallel translation in the manuscript *Leyenda de los Soles* (*Legend of the Suns*) [50] which was set down originally in 1558:

> *My flowers shall not perish*
> *Nor shall my chants cease,*
> *They spread, they scatter.*

Ah tlamiz noxochiuh ah tlamiz
  nocuic
In noconehua
Xexelihui ya moyahua

Mexico, like Peru, was a sun state. Above all was the sun god and no matter how many the manifestations of the gods, how widespread their influence, the sum of all things came from the sun. Mexico was virtually a Sun Kingdom.

> *Now our father the Sun*
> *Sinks attired in rich plumes,*
> *Within an urn of precious stones,*
> *As if girdled with turquoise necklaces goes,*
> *Among ceaselessly falling flowers. . . .*

Such is an idea, an idea, nothing more, of Aztec literature. It has recently been carefully scrutinized by Dr. Miguel León Portilla in a book, *La Filosofía Nahuatl* (not available in English), which casts a new light on the human qualities of the Aztec. There is more Aztec literature extant than one would at first surmise, even though much has been lost. But what *is* here tallies very well with what the first conquistadors said they saw of Aztec life and what has been confirmed by archaeology.

As the world spun in 1519, the Aztec could look back on a history which for sheer will to power has few peers. They came out of nothing and made themselves in a relatively short time heirs of thousands of years of culture even greater than their own, a culture which was adopted and assimilated by them. They gave the Mexican land its first direction toward some form of economic synthesis. They gave it a new concept of commerce by extending trade beyond traditional borders. Their knowledge of geography and of plants was vast. They developed paper into a veritable industry. They had writing which tended more and more to evolve into the phonetic. They had literature. They were using wooden and clay stamps to impress designs and symbols on their *amatl* paper. Thus the Aztec had all the ingredients—paper, writing, literature, and stamping—which ancient China had and which brought about the first steps toward that reproduction of ideas by printing which extended civilization.

It is, however, useless to speculate what might have been. In that year of 1519 a small fleet of vessels anchored at Vera Cruz: Hernán Cortés had arrived.

37. Hail and Farewell

THEY FELL.
It is a drama which, no matter how often told, never seems to lose the patina of its romance. The Spanish who took active part in it felt the historicity of the moment: Hernán Cortés penned his famous *Five Letters* even while wading through the sea of Aztec blood. Three other Spaniards who participated left their impressions as well, including that wonderful Bernal Díaz del Castillo, one who even at the age of eighty-four could not forget its impact: ". . . it all comes before my eyes as though it had happened but yesterday." The Conquest will be a source for literature for a long time and none perhaps will replace William Prescott's historical narrative. All the others that have followed—be it General Lew Wallace, D. H. Lawrence, or Samuel Shellabarger, or even Madariaga's *Heart of Jade* and Maurice Collis's *Cortés and Moctezuma*—are only pallid copies of the original piece forged by William Prescott.

They fell. Why they fell can be found in the literature—it was inevitable. Once white man began to probe into the new world, contact with the Aztecs and conquest of the Aztecs were a certainty; if it had not been Hernán Cortés, it would have been someone else.

Hernán Cortés, arrived at a psychological moment in Mexico (just as in Peru Francisco Pizarro came when the Incas had just gone through a civil war). A god, Quetzalcoatl, was expected from the east. Columbus made contact with the Mayas in his fourth and last voyage in 1502. This amazing bit of intelligence, enlarged every time it was told and retold, came to the ears of Aztec merchants who were trading near Yucatán at the ancient market of Xicalango at that time. Moctezuma came into power in 1503. During his reign white men continued to appear and disappear along the Gulf shores. Quetzalcoatl, the culture hero of these Americas, who was expelled from his land, vowed as he sailed away into that selfsame Gulf sea that "on the date of my birth which is Ce-Acatl, the year of 1-Reed—*I will return.*" According to the Aztec calendar this year 1-Reed could only fall, in the Christian calendar reckoning, in the years 1363, 1467, or 1519. In 1519 Hernán Cortés appeared on the shores of Vera Cruz, and one of the first gifts sent to him by Moctezuma was a magnificent headdress of quetzal plumes, the same headdress which today is in the Museum für Völkerkunde at Vienna. Long before this the whole Aztec people had gone through years of tribulations; they felt their insecurity as their priests searched the heavens and the earth for portents of disaster. Long columns of sacrificial victims were taken from tribute villages and immolated on the sacrificial block so that the gods might bring them answers to their questionings about the strange creatures that were appearing and disappearing on their shores. It was natural that these demands upon other tribes for sacrificial victims would alienate them; even those tribes who had been friendly for two hundred years were desperately angry over the drain on their own kin; bonds between conqueror and conquered were loosened. But the Aztecs in fear and uncertainty increased the pressure.

Then Hernán Cortés appeared. He came with new weapons, horses, steel armor, and new gods. Two different worlds, two different human natures, met. The Aztec had no concept of himself as a separate absolute entity; he thought in terms of clan. The Spaniard believed in his own person; the most real reality of his world was his own individual soul.[29]

They fell. They fell, suggests William Prescott, under the weight of a different, "if not in some respects higher, civilization; none of its achievements could save it and its own internal weaknesses helped to destroy it." Moral history is not good history; historical action, judged under the Spinozan "aspect of eternity," lies beyond good and evil. By its very nature history is amoral, and yet . . .

And yet what Prescott wrote bears some relation to the reality of the facts of this book: "The Aztec monarchy fell by the hand of its own subjects. . . . Its fate may serve as a striking proof that a government which does not rest on the sympathies of its subjects cannot long abide; that human institutions, when not connected with human prosperity and progress, must fall . . . by the hand of violence from within or from without."

Thus on Saint Hippolytus' Day, August 13, 1521, in the stench of a thousand fires, the Spanish Conquest was complete and the Aztec civilization passed into cultural limbo.

Bibliography

1. Acosta, José de, *The Naturall and Morall Historie of the East and West Indies*. London, 1604.
   A very learned and balanced Jesuit, whose intellectual love of God did not blind him to the good qualities of the Indian; this book is notable since it deals with Acosta's travels in Mexico and Peru as early as 1565. He compares the cultures, he is colorful and accurate. When obtained (which will be difficult) the work should be read.

2. Alzate y Ramírez, José Antonio, *Descripcion de las antiguedades de Xochicalco*. Mexico, 1791.
   Xochicalco was one of the first Mexican sites to enter the literature. Although Humboldt did not visit it, he gathered the description made by Señor Alzate with a drawing (something less than accurate) by F. Aguera done in 1791. This he published in his famous *Atlas Pittoresque* (Paris, 1810).

3. Anonymous Conqueror, *Narrative of Some Things of New Spain and of the Great City of Temestitan,* trans. by Marshall H. Saville. New York, 1917.
   Not easily available, since it has been reprinted in only limited editions, this short work by one who was anonymous and communal should be read alongside that of Bernal Díaz del Castillo and the letters of Cortés, to gain a full-sided picture of the impact of the Conquest on Aztec—and Spaniard.

4. Barrow, R. H., *The Romans*. Harmondsworth, England, 1949.

5. Boas, Franz (ed.), *General Anthropology*. Boston, 1938.

6. Borah, Woodrow, *Early Colonial Trade and Navigation Between Mexico and Peru*. Berkeley, Calif., 1954.

7. Brasseur de Bourbourg, C. E., *Historie des Nations Civilisées du Mexique et de l'Amérique Centrale*, 4 vols. Paris, 1857.

8. Burland, C. A., *Magic Books from Mexico*. London, 1953.

9. Caddy, Herbert, *City of Palenque*.
    This manuscript, illustrated with twenty-four sepia drawings, is unpublished. Caddy preceded Frederick Catherwood.

10. Calancha, Antonio de la, *Cronica moralizada del orden de San Augustin en el Perú* . . . Barcelona, 1638.

11. Caso, Alfonso, *Las Exploraciones en Monte Albán, Temporada 1934-35*. Instituto Panamericano de Geografía é Historia, no. 18. Mexico, 1935.
    One of the great figures in Mexican archaeology. His explorations into Monte Albán, an Olmec-Zapotec-Mixtec religious site in Oaxaca, and its restoration gave us more than fifteen hundred years of chronology. His discovery of the famous golden jewels at Monte Albán, in an untouched, unrifled tomb, gave the physical evidence of the excellence of Mexican goldsmithery.

12. ————, *El Pueblo del Sol*. Mexico, 1953.

13. Castañeda, Paganini Ricardo, *Las Ruinas de Palenque*. Guatemala, 1946.

14. Catherwood, Frederick, *Views of Ancient Monuments in Central America, Chiapas and Yucatan*. New York, 1844.

15. Chamberlain, Robert S., *Francisco de Montejo and the Conquest of Yucatán*, Ph.D. dissertation, Harvard University, 1936.

16. Childe, V. Gordon, "Early Forms of Society," in Singer, et al. (eds.), *A History of Technology*, vol. 1.

17. Cline, Howard F., "The Apocryphal Early Career of J. F. de Waldeck," *Acta Americana*, vol 4, no. 4 (1947).

18. *Codex Mendoza*, 2 vols. Mexico, 1925.

19. Collis, Maurice, *Cortés and Montezuma*. London, 1954.
    A recent interpretation, by a well-known English writer, of the strange relationship between Moctezuma and Hernán Cortés. Well guided by Aztec specialists, the author has given a new twist to the old facts.

20. Cornyn, John H. (trans. and ed.), "Aztec Literature," in *The Song of Quetzalcoatl*. Yellow Springs, Ohio, 1930.

21. Cortés, Hernán, *Five Letters, 1519–1526,* trans. by
    J. Bayard Morris. London, 1928; New York, 1929.
    The five letters were written between 1519 and 1526. In
    Spanish they were termed *Cartas-Relaciones,* half letters,
    half dispatches. These could not be called literary master-
    pieces; still, many were penned in the heat of battle—and
    bear this imprint. Two of them were published in 1524 in
    Nuremberg with the only plan of the city of Tenochtitlán
    as it was in 1519.

22. ———, *Letters of Cortes,* trans. and ed. by F. A. Mac-
    Nutt. New York, 1908.
    The originals of these letters are in the Nationalbibliothek
    in Vienna.

23. Covarrubias, Miguel, *Indian Art of Mexico and Central
    America.* New York, 1957.

24. ———, *Mexico South: The Isthmus of Tehuantepec.*
    New York, 1946.
    The late Miguel Covarrubias was by far and large more
    than a clever illustrator, he was an imaginative archaeolo-
    gist. He wandered much over the Mexican scene and pur-
    sued archaeology; his belief that the Olmec would emerge
    as one of the earliest of the Mexican tribes has been borne
    out by radiocarbon dating.

25. Díaz del Castillo, Bernal, *The Discovery and Conquest
    of Mexico, 1517–1521,* trans. by A. P. Maudslay. New
    York, 1956.
    Since it is an honest work and deals with people—the basic
    foundation of history—Bernal Díaz's book is a rich tapestry
    of human events. Its vitality is attested to by the continu-
    ously new editions that appear. Of the numerous editions,
    the one published recently in Mexico (1955) is the most
    complete and gives the whole of Díaz's travels with Cortés
    in the Maya country. I have used this edition as well as
    the Maudslay translation cited above.

26. Drucker, Philip, "Radiocarbon Dates from La Venta,
    Tabasco," *Science,* vol. 126, no. 3263 (July 12, 1957),
    72–3.

27. Durán, Fray Diego, *Historia de las Indias de Nueva-
    España* . . . 2 vols. and atlas. Mexico, 1867–80.
    Written in the sixteenth century.

28. Ekholm, Gordon F., *Excavations at Tampico and Pan-
    uco in the Huasteca, Mexico.* Anthropological Papers of

the American Museum of Natural History, vol. 38, pt.
5. New York, 1944.

29. Frank, Waldo, *America Hispaña: A Portrait and a Prospect*, New York, 1931.

30. Gamio, Lorenzo, *Archaeological Guide of Monte Albán*.
Mexico, n.d.

31. Gamio, Manuel, *La Población del Valle de Teotihuacán*,
3 vols. Mexico, 1922.

32. García, Gregorio, *Origen de los Indios . . .* Madrid,
1732.
This, written in 1607, is one of the many, albeit better-
known, theological proofs offered as to why the American
"Indians are Jewes." García identifies the Biblical Ophir
with Peru; Joktan of Genesis becomes Yucatán.

33. García Payón, "Malinalco," *Revista Mexicana de Estudios Antropologicos*, vol. VIII (1946).

34. Garibay, Kintana, Angel María, *Historia de la Literatura
Nahuatl*. Mexico, 1953.
A fascinating inquiry into the nature of Aztec literature, this
book shows the sensitive nature of a people renowned
mostly in human memory for their massive human sacrificial rituals. Sections appear in translation for the first
time in the Aztec part of the present volume.

35. Gates, William (trans.), *The de la Cruz-Badiano Aztec
Herbal of 1552*. Baltimore, 1939.

36. Hernández, Francisco, *Rerum Medicarum Novae Hispaniae Thesaurus seu Plantarum*. Rome, 1649.
The work of the great Spanish proto-medico Francisco Her-
nández, who came to Mexico during the years 1570-75. With
his Aztec assistants, he filled sixteen folio volumes with
drawings of three thousand plants and descriptions in
Spanish, Nahuatl, and Latin. Reduced to one thousand
species, the book was a gigantic herbal on Dioscoridean
lines. Unpublished in his lifetime, this badly edited thesaurus
of 951 pages was printed in Rome.
   See also: von Hagen, "Francisco Hernández: Naturalist,
   1515–1578."

37. Heyerdahl, Thor, *Kon-Tiki: Across the Pacific by Raft*,
trans. by F. H. Lyon, Chicago, 1951.

38. Holmes, William H., *Archaeological Studies Among the*

Ancient Cities of Mexico. Field Columbian Museum, Pubs. 8, 16. Chicago, 1895–97.

39. Hooke, H. S., "Recording and Writing," in Singer, et al. (eds.), *A History of Technology,* vol. 1.

40. Humboldt, Alexander von, *Vues des Cordillères et Monuments des Peuples Indigènes de l'Amérique,* Paris, 1810. Humboldt was the great figure of the opening of the nineteenth century. After explorations in South America, Cuba, and Mexico, he compiled a vast amount of data extraordinary in both its range and its accuracy. This work is a landmark in American archaeology but now little used since the volume is in folio and is expensive. Yet it deserves to be reconsidered. His attitude toward archaeological remains as fragments of history laid the solid base of American scholarship. He was the first to stress the oneness of indigenous culture.

41. Hunter, Dard, *Chinese Ceremonial Paper,* Chillicothe, Ohio, 1937.

42. ———, *Papermaking: The History and Technique of an Ancient Craft,* 2nd ed. rev. and enl. New York, 1947.

43. Huxley, Aldous, *Beyond the Mexique Bay.* New York, 1934.
A charming small book on the effect of Middle America and Mexico on Aldous Huxley. All of the conclusions are Huxleian, always stimulating and with a slant which the professional scholar has not seen or does not see.

44. Ixtililoxochitl, Fernando de Alva, *Obras Históricas . . . ,* 2 vols. Mexico, 1891–92.
Written in the seventeenth century.

45. Jones, Sir Harold Spencer, "The Calendar," in Singer, et al. (eds.), *A History of Technology,* vol. 3.

46. Joyce, T. A., *Mexican Archaeology.* London and New York, 1914.
A very successful attempt to portray the whole of the field of Mexican archaeology. A rare book when obtainable, and expensive.

47. Kelemen, Pál, *Medieval American Art,* 2 vols. New York, 1943.
This, the mature work of a Hungarian-born and -educated art historian, has a freshness and directness not always found in literature on the Maya and Aztec. He treats the objects as art, not as potsherds; his observations, since they

are neither hipped nor dulled by the standard archaeological
vocabulary, are thought-evoking. It should be read by any
who wish to push their interest in American cultures beyond
the dim outline of general books.

48. King, Edward, Viscount Kingsborough, *Antiquities of
Mexico*, 9 vols. London, 1831–48.
Lord Kingsborough would have been sunk in the stream
of time except that he published, at the cost of both life
and fortune, this folio collection of nine volumes at $150 a
copy. The set is now eagerly sought by collectors and
scholars since Lord Kingsborough reproduced many of the
heretofore unpublished Mixtec, Aztec, and Maya codices.
The text, which is a ragbag of every unconsidered theory,
attempts to prove in short that the American Indian de-
scended from one of the Lost Tribes of Israel. He belonged
to the lunatic fringe of archaeological enthusiasts. He died,
quite undeservedly, in debtors' prison, because of his failure
to pay for the paper that was used in this publication.
Kingsborough belongs to history, but his history scarcely
belongs to him.

49. Kirchhoff, "Mesoamerica," *Acta Americana,* vol. 1
(1943).

50. León Portilla, Miguel, *La Filosofía Nahuatl.* Mexico,
1956.
An unusually profound and thoroughly documented work
using the remains of the Aztec literature to suggest the complex Aztec interest in the world about him. The selection
of the material, its elucidation through actual Aztec texts,
provides another aspect of Aztec life, otherwise missing in
the literature about them.

51. L'Éstrange, Hamon, *Americans no Iewes* . . . London,
1652.

52. Lévy-Bruhl, Lucien, *Primitives and the Supernatural,*
trans. by Lilian A. Clare. New York, 1935.

53. Linné, Sigvald, *Archaeological Researches at Teotihuacán, Mexico.* New York and London, 1934.

54. López de Gómara, Francisco; *Cronica de la Nueva-
España, con la Conquista de Mexica* . . . *hechos por el
valeroso Hernando Cortés, Marqués del Valle.* Zaragoza,
1552.

55. Lothrop, Samuel K., "South America as Seen from
Middle America," in *The Maya and Their Neighbors.*

56. Madariaga, Salvador de, *Hernán Cortés, Conquerer of Mexico*. New York, 1941.

57. Mangelsdorf, Paul, *Races of Maize in Mexico*. Cambridge, 1956.

58. Marquina, Ignacio, *Arquitectura Prehispánica*. Mexico, 1951.

59. Mason, John Alden, "Native Languages of Middle America," in *The Maya and Their Neighbors*.

60. Maudslay, Anne Cary and A. P., *A Glimpse at Guatemala*, London, 1899.

61. Morley, Sylvanus G., *The Ancient Maya*. Palo Alto, Calif., 1946.

62. Motolinía, Toribio de Benavente o, *Historia de los Indios de la Nueva España*. Barcelona, 1914.
    Written in the sixteenth century.

63. ———, *Vocabulario*. Mexico, 1555.

64. Neugebauer, O. "Ancient Mathematics and Astronomy," in Singer, et al. (eds.), *A History of Technology*, vol. 1.

65. Noguera, Eduardo, *Cerámica de México*. Mexico, 1932.

66. Nuttall, Zelia (trans. and ed.), *Codex Magliabecchi: The Book of Life of the Ancient Mexicans, Containing an Account of Their Rites and Superstitions*. Berkeley, Calif., 1903.

67. Prescott, William H., *History of the Conquest of Mexico*. New York, 1843.
    This work has withstood a century of siege, from all quarters. It still remains, since Prescott worked from original sources and knew how to thread his way between fact and fiction, the best over-all history of the Conquest of Mexico. New material has altered it, new evidence and discoveries have augmented it, but it remains the master work.

68. Sahagún, Bernardino de, *A History of Ancient Mexico*, trans. by Fanny R. Bandelier. Nashville, Tenn., 1932.
    Sahagún came early to Mexico (1595) while the Aztec traditions were still alive. The work is wonderfully detailed (there are accompanying illustrations which do not appear in all the publications) and it is an honest attempt at reportage. The edition in English was prepared by Fanny

Bandelier, the widow of Adolph Bandelier, one of the pioneers in American Indian studies.

69. ———, *Historia General de las Cosas de Nueva España,* 3 vols. Mexico, 1938.

70. Sapper, Karl Theodor, *Das Nördliche Mittel-Amerika.* Braunschweig, 1897.

71. Sauer, Carl O., "Cultivated Plants of South and Central America," in Steward (ed.), *Handbook of South American Indians,* vol. 6.

72. Saville, Marshall H., *Tizoc, Great Lord of the Aztecs, 1481–1486.* Museum of the American Indian, Contributions from the Heye Museum, vol. 7. New York, 1929.

73. Sorensen, John L., "Some Mesoamerican Traditions of Immigration," *El México Antiguo,* vol. VIII (1955), 425–39.

74. Soustelle, Jacques, *La Vida Cotidiana de los Aztecas.* Mexico, 1955. *La Vie Quotidienne des Aztèques à la Veille de la Conquête Espagnole.* Paris, 1955.
Pre-Conquest and later post-Conquest reportorial drawings of the Aztecs tell their own story. Written by a Frenchman, very expert in his field, with a new presentation, the book is available in French and Spanish, not yet in English.

75. Spengler, Oswald, *The Decline of the West,* 2 vols., trans. by Charles F. Atkinson. New York, 1927-28.

76. Stephens, John Lloyd, *Incidents of Travel in Central America, Chiapas, and Yucatan,* 2 vols. New York, 1841.
This work is to all intents and purposes the first recording of the discovery of the great extent of the Mayas. With its accurate yet dramatic drawings by Frederick Catherwood, it was a pioneering work. A reprint is now available (1 vol., ed. by Richard L. Predmore, New Brunswick, N. J., 1949) and a two-volume edition is shortly to appear (ed. with notes by von Hagen, Norman, Okla.).
See also: von Hagen, *Maya Explorer* and *Frederick Catherwood, Architect.*

77. Stirling, Matthew W., "La Venta" in *An Initial Series from Tres Zapotes, Vera Cruz, Mexico.* Contributed Technical Papers of the National Geographic Society, Mexican Archaeology Series, vol. 1, no. 1. Washington, D. C., 1940.

78. Tapia, Andres de, *Relación hecha por Andres de Tapia sobre la Conquista de México*. Colección de Documentos para la Historia de México, vol. 11. Mexico, 1866.

79. *Tenayuca Official Guide*. Mexico, n.d.

80. Thompson, J. Eric S., *Mexico Before Cortez*. New York, 1933.

81. Vaillant, George C., *The Aztecs of Mexico*. New York, 1941.
    One of the first archaeological histories of the Aztec, and still the most complete. It was written by the best-grounded of all the present-day scholars and although written for the general reader, it suggests the method of Vaillant's thinking.

82. Villa Rojas, Alfonso, *The Yaxuna-Cobá Causeway*. Carnegie Institution of Washington, Pub. 436. Washington, D. C., 1934.

83. Volney, Constantin, *Les Ruines: ou Méditation sur les Révolutions des Empires*. Paris, 1791.
    There is an edition in English of *The Ruins* which was prepared by Count Volney himself. Although the book is rhapsodic and, as archaeology, inaccurate, still it had great influence in France, England, and the United States. It provided at this early date (1791) much stimulus toward interest in man's past.

84. von Hagen, Victor Wolfgang, *The Aztec and Maya Papermakers*. New York, 1943.
    There are three editions of this work, the first book on the subject. The 1943 edition was limited to 220 copies and contained actual samples of bark paper. Another edition published the following year from the same type has been better proofread, but lacks the paper samples. A superb edition, limited to 750 copies, was issued in Mexico (*La Fabricación del Papel entre los Aztecas y los Mayas*, 1945).
        See also: von Hagen, "Mexican Papermaking Plants" and "Paper and Civilization."

85. ———, "Francisco Hernández: Naturalist, 1515-1578," *Scientific Monthly*, vol. 58 (May, 1944), 383–5.

86. ———, *Frederick Catherwood, Architect*. New York, 1950.

87. ———, *Highway of the Sun*. New York, 1955.

88. ———, *Jungle in the Clouds*. New York, 1940.

89. ————, *Maya Explorer: John Lloyd Stephens and the Lost Cities of Central America and Yucatán.* Norman, Okla., 1947.

90. ————, "Mexican Papermaking Plants," *Journal of the New York Botanical Gardens,* vol. 44, 1943.

91. ————, "Paper and Civilization," *Scientific Monthly,* vol. 57 (October, 1943), 301–14.

92. ————, *South America Called Them: Explorations of the Great Naturalists: La Condamine, Humboldt, Darwin, Spruce.* New York, 1945.

93. ————, "Waldeck," *Natural History,* vol. 55 (December, 1946), 450–6.

94. Wagner, Henry R., *The Rise of Fernando Cortés.* Berkeley, Calif., 1944.

95. Waldeck, J. F. de, *Voyage Pittoresque et Archéologue, dans la Province d'Yucatán . . .* Paris, 1838.
That which Humboldt put forward, Waldeck retarded. Humboldt compiled evidence as to the American origin of the Indian; Waldeck, a brilliant draftsman, falsified Maya figures and hieroglyphics and gave "substances" to the vague theory of the Jewish origin of the American Indian. His title of "Count" was bogus, his personal history in great part an invention. We know that he lived in Paris, managed a silver mine at Tlalpujahna and painted backdrops for the stage in Mexico, traveled in Yucatán and visited Palenque. The book is beautiful, facile, and contrived.
For critical appraisal of Waldeck, see also: von Hagen, "Waldeck"; and Cline, "The Apocryphal Early Career of J. F. de Waldeck."

96. Zeuner, F. E., "Cultivation of Plants," in Singer, et al. (eds.), *A History of Technology,* vol. 1.

Chronology

Europe and North America	AZTEC
c. 2000 B.C. *Greeks active in Troy.*	c. 2000 B.C. "Tepexpan Man" valley of Mexico; bones associated with mammoth elephants.
850 B.C. *Age of Homer.*	
776 B.C. *First Olympiad held in Greece.*	800 B.C.–A.D. c. 600 Olmecs. La Venta culture in Mexico hotlands.
753 B.C. *Legendary founding of Rome.*	
	500 B.C.–A.D. 1469 Monte Albán. Large stone temple-city in Oaxaca. Goes through five stages of culture and growth over two-thousand-year period.
	c. 500 B.C. The formative period of many highland and lowland cultures: Teotihaucán, Olmec, Huastec, Monte Albán, early Totonac.
431–404 B.C. *Peloponnesian Wars.*	c. 500 B.C. *Tlachtli* (a form of basketball) invented by Olmecs. *Tlachtli* spreads to tribes from Arizona to Nicaragua.
331 B.C. *Alexander the Great defeats Darius at Arbela.*	

c. 240 B.C. *Eratosthenes computes the size of the earth.*

146 B.C. *Romans capture and destroy Carthage.*

44 B.C. *Assassination of Julius Caesar.*

A.D. 79 *Volcanic Destruction of Herculaneum and Pompeii.*

c. 117 *Roman Empire at its greatest extent.*

235 *Disintegration of Roman Empire.*

337 *Death of Constantine.*

400–800 *The Mound Builders: Wisconsin to Gulf of Mexico.*

410 *Alaric sacks Rome.*

500 *Pueblo Indian culture begins in Utah, Colorado, Arizona.*

529 *Publication of the Justinian Code.*

632 *Death of Mohammed.*

800 *Imperial Coronation of Charlemagne at Rome.*

871–899 *Alfred, king of Wessex and of England.*

200 B.C. First evidence of Toltec culture in the valley of Anáhuac.

31 B.C. First known dated Olmec monument. Inventors of glyph writing, which spreads throughout Mexico and Maya country.

c. A.D. 100 Sun Temple at Teotihuacán is built (Chimalhuacan phase).

c. 200 Monte Albán (Period 1) in Oaxaca.

c. 400 Monte Albán rebuilt, extended (Zapotec period).

510 Toltecs, under "king" Chalciuh Tlanetzin begin to build temples of the Sun and Moon at Teotihuacán.

770 Teotihuacán Period II. Mitl-Tlacomihua, chief of Toltecs, builds temple to Quetzalcoatl.

c. 890 Great drought. Period of decline of Teotihuacán.

Europe and North America	*AZTEC*
900 *Golden Age of Arabian power in Spain.*	900 Xochicalco, a temple-city (south of Cuernavaca), built by the Toltecs. Tula, new center of Toltecs, is built.
	967 Ce Acatl Topiltzin takes name of the god Quetzalcoatl, rules Tula for 20 years.
c. 985 *Vikings settle Greenland.*	987 Quetzalcoatl, exiled from Tula, moves southwest toward Yucatán with large body of warriors.
1066–87 *William I (the conqueror), king of England.*	
	1156 Tula destroyed by Chichimecs. Another migration of Toltecs results. They settle at Xicalango.
1189–92 *Third Crusade, Frederick Barbarossa, Richard the Lion-Hearted, and Philip II.*	1168 Aztec history begins. Migratory tribes enter valley of Anáhuac.
1227 *Death of Genghis Khan.*	
1275 *Five-year drought in American Southwest. Raid by Navaho brings end to Cliff Dweller culture.*	1250 Aztecs, called Tenochas, living in area about Chapultepec close to Lake Texcoco.
	c. 1325 Aztecs occupy two islets in Lake Texcoco. Tenochtitlán, "Place of the Tenocha," is founded.
1347 *Black Death spreads through Europe.*	
1386 *Chaucer composes the* Canterbury Tales.	1375 Acamapichtli, first historical "king," or Chief Speaker, of the Tenochas.
	1395 Huitzilhuitl, second in line, begins to enlarge his capital.

1415 *Henry V defeats French at Agincourt.*

1414 Chimalpopoca elected Chief Speaker by the noble *tlatoani,* the electors of Aztec rulers.

1431 *Joan of Arc burned at the stake.*

1428 Izcoatl, born a slave, rises to leadership. Tenochas assume Aztec civilization. Izcoatl orders all previous historical picture paintings to be destroyed. Begins systematic wars on all neighboring tribes.

1440 Moctezuma I elected Chief Speaker.

1441–56 Drought. Crop failures, snow, frost.

1450–55 *The Gutenberg Bible.*

1453 *Fall of Constantinople.*

1469 *Union of ruling houses of Castile and Aragon through marriage of Ferdinand and Isabella.*

1469 Axayacatl succeeds his father Moctezuma I. Extends conquest to Isthmus of Tehuantepec. Campaigns into Tarascan territory, suffers sharp defeat.

1481 Tizoc succeeds his brother Axayacatl. Begins construction of great temple to Huitzilopochtli, the Aztec War God.

1481 Great sacrificial stone carved. Calendar stone set up. Recovered in 1790.

1483 *Richard III, last of Plantagenet kings of England, begins reign.*

1486 Ahuitzotl succeeds his brother Tizoc. Dedicates temple to Huitzilopochtli by immolating 20,000 sacrificial victims. Extends conquests down into Pacific side of Guatemala. *Pochteca* merchants in Honduras, Nicaragua.

1492 *Columbus discovers America.*

1497 *North America discovered by John Cabot.*

1498 *Columbus discovers mainland of South America.*

1500 *Birth of Benvenuto Cellini.*

1503 Moctezuma II, grandson of other of same name, elected Chief Speaker.

1507 New Fire ceremony. Columbus' presence in 1503 reported. Priests believe end of world is near.

1513 *Juan Ponce de León discovers Florida.*

1519 *Magellan begins circumnavigation of the globe.*

1519 Cortés enters Tenochtitlán. Captures Moctezuma.

1520 Moctezuma stoned and killed by own people.

1520 Cuitlahuac is made Leader, dies in melee as Spaniards fight their way out of Tenochtitlán.

1521 Cuauhtémoc is named last Chief Speaker. Defends Mexico against Cortés. Tenochtitlán falls to conquistadors.

1524 Cortés marches through Tabasco, Campeche, into El Petén in order to subdue an unauthorized colony in Honduras.

1525 Cuauhtémoc taken as hostage. He is hanged in the Maya province of Acalán.

1525 End of Aztec Empire.

1529 *First siege of Vienna by the Turks.*

1534 *Church of England established.*

1539–42 *Hernando De Soto explores the Mississippi.*

1547 *Death of Henry VIII.*

1565 *Ivan the Terrible of Russia initiates reign of terror.*

1579 *Francis Drake explores California coast.*

1588 *Defeat of Spanish Armada.*

1620 *Plymouth Colony established in Massachusetts.*

1675–76 *King Philip's War in New England.*

1680 *Pueblo revolt in Nuevo Mexico.*

1733 *Molasses Act stirs up English colonies.*

1748 *Excavations at Pompeii begin.*

1776 *Declaration of Independence by the Thirteen Colonies.*

INDEX